Key Stage Three

Religious Education

This CGP book is for pupils studying Religious Education at
Key Stage Three (ages 11-14). It's also an excellent introduction
for students planning to take Religious Studies at GCSE.

Inside, you'll find clear, comprehensive study notes covering
Christianity, **Judaism**, **Islam**, **Hinduism**, **Buddhism** and **Sikhism**.

At the end of each section, we've included a range of practice questions
to test students on their knowledge and understanding.

Complete Study and Practice

Section One — Looking for God

Section Two — Key Religious Figures

Section Three — Beliefs and Practice

Contents

Published by CGP

Editors:
Ben Ffrancon Davies
Rachel Grocott
Lucy Loveluck
Holly Poynton
Matt Topping

Contributors:
Mark Craster-Chambers, Jill Hudson, Hugh Mascetti, Duncan Raynor, Paul Smith, Cavan Wood

With thanks to Glenn Rogers and Philip West for the proofreading.

ISBN: 978 1 78294 185 9

With thanks to Jan Greenway for the copyright research.

Scripture quotations (marked NIV) taken from the Holy Bible, New International Version Anglicised
Copyright © 1979, 1984, 2011 Biblica
Used by permission of Hodder & Stoughton Ltd, an Hachette UK company.
All rights reserved.
'NIV' is a registered trademark of Biblica.
UK trademark number 1448790.

Holy Qur'an quotations taken from the Holy Qur'an, Sahih International Version
www.quran.com

With thanks to Enid Thompson for the church photos on page 68.

Every effort has been made to locate copyright holders and obtain permission to reproduce sources. For those
sources where it has been difficult to trace the originator of the work, we would be grateful for information.
If any copyright holder would like us to make an amendment to the acknowledgements, please notify us
and we will gladly update the book at the next reprint. Thank you.

Printed by Elanders Ltd, Newcastle upon Tyne.
Clipart from Corel®

Based on the classic CGP style created by Richard Parsons.

The Nature of Truth

Sometimes it's not as simple as just saying that something is true or false. There are different types of truth, and different people can interpret even the same type of truth in different ways...

There are **Different** types of **Truth**

1) Here are five different types of truth:

Aesthetic Truth

This is the kind of truth that you find in films or novels. What's happening isn't actually true, but it can be realistic and believable.

Historical Truth

These are facts about what happened in the past. We have evidence for these facts, even though we weren't there to witness them first hand. For example, we know that Henry VIII had six wives even though we never met them.

Moral Truth

This refers to things that we know are right or wrong. For example, we know that it is wrong to take something that isn't ours.

Scientific Truth

This is information about how the natural world works. It is supported by scientific experiments.

Religious Truth

This is truth about the ultimate meaning and purpose of life and the Universe, especially as it relates to people's faiths and beliefs.

2) Religious truths can be interpreted in different ways and more than one interpretation can be valid.

3) For example, all Christians believe the story of creation contains religious truth. Some also believe it is historically true (they believe that it actually took place), while others do not.

Not Everyone Believes in a god

When it comes to religious truths, there are three main ways to categorise people's beliefs:

1) A theist is someone who believes that a god (or gods) exists — this belief is called theism. Theists often believe God created the world.

2) An atheist is someone who believes that a god (or gods) doesn't exist — this belief is called atheism.

3) An agnostic is someone who believes that there's no way of being sure whether a god (or gods) exists — this belief is called agnosticism.

Some truths are easily believable, but some aren't...

It's pretty easy to believe something when you've got hard evidence to convince you. But persuading someone to believe in a god that you can't see or hear can be a lot harder.

Origins of the World

Different <u>religions</u> have different beliefs about the <u>origins</u> of the world.

Christians believe that *God* created *Everything*

1) Some believe that the account in Genesis should be taken <u>literally</u>. They believe that the process took six days and that humankind did not evolve from apes, but descended from Adam and Eve. This is called <u>creationism</u>. Christians who believe in creationism <u>reject</u> the scientific account of evolution.

2) Some Christians accept both the Bible <u>and</u> the scientific account of evolution — some believe that the creation story is a <u>simplified</u> description of evolution.

3) Others believe that the creation story is <u>not historical</u> at all, but still contains <u>religious truth</u> about the <u>importance</u> of human beings and the world.

> "In the beginning God created the heavens and the earth." Genesis 1:1 NIV

> The Bible says things were created in the following order — the heavens (i.e. space) and Earth, the sea, atmosphere and land, and then plants, animals and people. This is similar to the way scientists believe things appeared. So the timescale is different (millions of years rather than six days), but the general idea is the same.

Jews interpret the story of *Creation* in *Different* ways

1) Christian and Jewish ideas about creation come from the <u>same</u> scriptures, so they're quite <u>similar</u>.

2) Many <u>Orthodox</u> Jews accept <u>theistic evolution</u> — this means they accept <u>both</u> the <u>creation story and evolution</u> — so they think that G-d created the world using evolution.

3) Many <u>Reform</u> Jews believe that the creation story tells us that G-d <u>created everything</u>, but not <u>how</u> it was created.

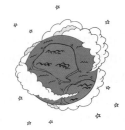

Some Islamic ideas can Exist Side-By-Side *with science*

1) Muslims believe that <u>Allah</u> created the world and everything in it.

2) However, unlike Christianity and Judaism, descriptions of <u>creation</u> in the Qur'an are not entirely at odds with science. In fact, scientific theories are often <u>supported</u> by passages such as this.

3) When scientific theories and the teachings of the Qur'an <u>disagree</u>, Muslims believe that the Qur'an's word is the <u>truth</u>.

> "Have those who disbelieved not considered that the heavens and the earth were a joined entity, and We separated them and made from water every living thing? Then will they not believe?" Qur'an 21:30

Most religious people believe that God created the whole world

Christianity, Judaism and Islam all teach that God created the Earth. But the details of the creation accounts differ, and can be interpreted in different ways, even within each religion.

The Design Argument

The <u>argument from design</u> is one of the main arguments for the existence of a creator god.

"*Someone* must have *Designed* the Universe"

1) The <u>argument from design</u> is that the <u>intricate workings</u> of the <u>Universe</u> (or of <u>life</u>) <u>can't</u> have come about by <u>chance</u>. There must have been some kind of <u>designer</u> — and this designer was <u>God</u>.

2) Design arguments include Isaac Newton's <u>Thumb Theory</u> and William Paley's <u>Watchmaker Theory</u>:

The Thumb Theory

Every <u>thumbprint</u> is intricate and <u>unique</u>, so someone must have designed them. In this case, there must be a creator — a god.

The Watchmaker Theory

Some philosophers argue that you <u>wouldn't think</u> an <u>intricate watch</u> you found was made <u>by chance</u> — so why believe the <u>world was</u>?

4) Even Albert Einstein, an important scientist (and an agnostic — see p.1), said: "When I see all the glories of the cosmos, I can't help but believe that there is a <u>divine hand</u> behind it all."

5) Einstein might have been talking about the <u>design</u> of the Universe, but he might instead have been talking about a <u>numinous</u> experience (see p.7) he had while thinking about it.

Mr Einstein

Not everybody is **Convinced** *by the* **Design Argument**

1) If a god created <u>everything</u>, this would include all the <u>suffering</u> that has a <u>natural cause</u> (see p.102), such as <u>natural disasters</u> and <u>disease</u>. Some people find it hard to believe that a good and loving god would create such <u>terrible</u> things.

2) Some people dismiss the design argument because there is no real <u>proof</u> that God made the Universe — there certainly aren't any <u>witnesses</u>.

3) Others question <u>what</u> or <u>who designed God</u> if God designed everything.

4) <u>Buddhists</u> don't believe a god created the Universe. They also think it's <u>illogical</u> to compare the creation of something as complex as the Universe to something <u>man-made</u>.

"*The world is too complex to have just randomly appeared.*"

This is a tricky one to form an opinion on — nobody knows for sure how the Universe got to be as complex as it is, but the design argument has convinced many people that God exists.

The Cosmological Argument

The <u>cosmological</u> argument suggests that there was a '<u>First Cause</u>' that resulted in the creation of the Universe — some people believe that this first cause was <u>God</u>.

"There must have been a *First Cause*"

1) The Universe as we know it works on the principle of '<u>cause and effect</u>' — that is, <u>everything</u> that happens is <u>caused</u> by something else.

2) So an event happening <u>now</u> was caused by an <u>earlier</u> event, which in turn was caused by an even earlier event and so on back through time.

3) That means there are <u>two possibilities</u> for the beginning of the Universe:

   a) The chain goes back forever — i.e. the Universe has <u>always</u> existed; it's eternal.

   b) You eventually reach a starting point — an <u>uncaused cause</u> or '<u>First Cause</u>'.

4) Some people argue that the 'First Cause' in the creation of the Universe must have been <u>God</u>.

Not Everyone Accepts the cosmological argument

1) One argument is "Why doesn't the 'First Cause' need a cause if everything else does?" — the existence of a god <u>doesn't agree</u> with the idea that <u>everything</u> is <u>caused</u> by something else.

2) Some people argue that if God doesn't need a cause and '<u>just exists</u>', why can't the Universe '<u>just exist</u>' without a cause?

3) Other nonbelievers argue that just because a 'First Cause' <u>exists</u>, it doesn't have to be a <u>god</u>.

The *Big Bang Theory* suggests another 'First Cause'

1) Some people argue that the <u>Big Bang theory</u> offers an <u>alternative</u> 'First Cause'.

2) According to this scientific theory, both <u>space</u> and <u>time</u> started with the <u>Big Bang</u> (an explosion of matter and energy). Matter from this explosion eventually formed <u>stars</u>, <u>planets</u> and <u>everything</u> else.

3) If this is true, then asking what 'caused' the Big Bang is <u>meaningless</u> — causes only happen in time, and time only started with the Big Bang.

4) Although this theory is often used to argue that <u>no</u> divine being exists, many religious people believe the story of creation and the Big Bang theory can both be true. They think God could be <u>responsible</u> for the Big Bang and used it, with evolution, as his way of creating the Universe.

5) In 1996, the <u>Roman Catholic Church</u> officially accepted the Big Bang theory which was seen as a significant <u>acceptance</u> of science.

The 'First Cause' wasn't caused by anything

So, that's another interesting theory that's been put together to try to explain what we're all doing here. I can tell you what *we're* doing here next — learning about evolution, so read on.

Evolution and Religion

The theory of evolution can make it <u>hard</u> for some people to <u>believe</u> that a god exists.

Darwin argued that we Evolved from Apes

1) In 1859, <u>Charles Darwin</u> published 'On the Origin of Species'. In this book, he argued that all life on the planet originated from <u>simple cells</u>.

2) Life <u>evolved</u> (gradually changed) over millions of years into a huge variety of forms. According to this theory, we evolved from <u>apes</u> — not from Adam and Eve.

3) The theory of evolution suggests that the most useful <u>characteristics</u> get passed on to the next generation through <u>natural selection</u>.

4) Beings that possess useful characteristics are more likely to <u>survive</u> and <u>reproduce</u> — for example, lizards with effective <u>camouflage</u> are more likely to survive than those without.

5) Some people argue that natural selection is responsible for <u>moral behaviour</u> — being kind to someone generally makes them less likely to hurt you, so it's a <u>survival</u> instinct.

People Interpret Evolution in different ways

1) At first, many people were <u>upset</u> by Darwin's theory. Some Christians felt that it <u>threatened</u> their faith — if the <u>Bible</u> was <u>wrong</u> about how humans were created, then it could be wrong about other things too.

2) <u>Creationists</u> (people who take the creation story in Genesis <u>literally</u>) still <u>dismiss</u> the theory of evolution.

3) However, many <u>theists</u> (see p.1) believe in <u>theistic evolution</u> — they accept both evolution and the creation of the world by God (see p.2).

> Some Muslims believe in <u>theistic evolution</u> because it can explain what the Qur'an doesn't mention — therefore giving them a better <u>understanding</u> of Allah.

> Science doesn't explain why the world was created or why we're all here. Some people look to religion for answers to these questions.

'Theistic evolution' means that a god is responsible for evolution

It's hard to know what to believe with all these theories flying about the place — but you can't deny that it's pretty intriguing. Have a think about why people believe each of these theories.

The Meaning of Life

"Why are we here?" — people have been debating this question for thousands of years. Science gives no answer to this question, but religion tries to provide one.

Religion gives a Reason for our lives on Earth

1) Christians believe that God created us to have a relationship with him. He loves us and enjoyed creating us.

2) Some verses of the Bible suggest that God created us to look after the rest of his creation. This theory is called stewardship and is supported by the Bible: ➡️

> "The Lord God took the man and put him in the Garden of Eden to work it and take care of it." Genesis 2:15 NIV

3) Many Christians, Jews and Muslims believe that what happens after our deaths (see p.88-90) depends on how we lived. So the purpose of us being here now might be some sort of test — of our morals or faith.

4) One of Allah's names is al-Hakeem, which means 'the most wise' — Muslims don't believe that Allah would create anything that doesn't have a valid purpose. They believe that Allah created humans to serve and worship him.

> "And I did not create... mankind except to worship Me." Qur'an 51:56

There's no Scientific reason for us being here

1) Science doesn't deal with the idea of purpose. It has worked out how we got here — by the process of evolution — but says nothing about why we're here.

2) Science explains 'special' human characteristics, e.g. kindness, as things that have evolved to help us survive (e.g. if you help someone in need, they're more likely to help you in return).

3) Science sees human beings as simply another type of animal — just a very brainy type.

Muslims believe that everything Allah created has a purpose

Creation and the purpose of life are hot topics for debate. There's no scientific reason for us being here, so religious explanations for life on Earth are attractive to many people.

Reasons for Belief: Revelation

Millions of people across the world believe in some kind of <u>divine being</u> or <u>god</u>. Some people are <u>brought up</u> to believe in a god, but others start to believe for a variety of <u>different</u> reasons.

People **Believe** for **Different Reasons**

1) Some people believe in a god because they are brought up by <u>religious parents</u>.

2) Some people <u>choose</u> to follow a religion when they see how religion <u>helps</u> people who are <u>suffering</u> all over the world.

3) The <u>search for meaning</u> is a major reason why some people become interested in religion. People want to find <u>answers</u>, and they believe religion can help.

Revelation may lead to **Belief** in a god

1) Religious believers think God shows his <u>existence</u> to us in a variety of ways.

2) This showing is called <u>revelation</u> because it shows something that is usually <u>hidden</u>.

3) Revelation can be <u>general</u> (available to <u>everyone</u>) or <u>special</u> (an <u>individual</u> experience), and there are many different types.

4) Here are some <u>examples</u> of revelation:

> 1) SACRED TEXTS: Christians, Muslims and Jews believe that the <u>truth</u> about the world was <u>revealed</u> to them by God. These revelations were written down in the <u>scriptures</u> — the Bible (p.42-43), the Qur'an (p.46-47) and the Torah (p.44-45).
>
> 2) CONSCIENCE AND MORALITY: Human beings know the difference between <u>right</u> and <u>wrong</u>, and have <u>free will</u>. Some people believe that a god must exist to have given us these abilities.
>
> 3) RELIGIOUS LEADERS: God can reveal himself through the <u>acts</u> of religious leaders. If a religious leader can accomplish something <u>great</u> to help others, then maybe <u>God</u> is on their side. Many believers also think that God <u>speaks</u> to them through their religious leaders — giving them <u>moral guidance</u>.
>
> 4) NUMINOUS EXPERIENCES: This is where something inspires <u>awe</u> and <u>wonder</u> in a person — so that they can feel God's presence. For example, a beautiful sunset, a wild sea or a butterfly's wing might <u>convince</u> people that there must be a <u>creator</u>.

There are lots of reasons for belief

Basically, religion's a personal thing — Abi believes because her mum does, Sam gazes at the stars at night and reckons there must be a god, and Al doesn't believe in God at all.

Reasons for Belief: Revelation

Religious believers think that God <u>reveals</u> himself to them so that they can <u>know</u> him.

Revelation can be **Messages** *from* **God**...

Believers might feel like they've received a <u>message</u> from God in a number of different ways:

1) VISIONS: A believer might think they have '<u>seen</u>' God.

2) PROPHESYING: A believer might <u>speak a message</u> from God.

3) SPEAKING IN TONGUES: This is linked to prophesying — some believers might begin '<u>speaking in tongues</u>' (unknown languages) — they believe they're speaking God's words.

4) DREAMS: Sometimes, God reveals himself to a person in a <u>dream</u>. They might feel that something in their dream was a <u>message</u> from God telling them <u>what</u> to do.

During prayer or meditation, Charismatic Christian worshippers often believe that they are receiving messages from God.

...*Or a* **Feeling** *that* **God** *is* **Present**

Revelation can be more focused on the <u>feeling</u> that God is there:

1) PRAYER: A person might feel the presence of God while praying, or in an <u>answered prayer</u>, for example if an ill person they pray for is cured.

2) SACRAMENTAL RITUALS: Some Christians believe that God makes his presence felt directly during sacramental rituals. For example, in the <u>Eucharist</u> (Mass or Holy Communion — a service where bread and wine is blessed and shared).

3) MIRACLES: When an extraordinary event cannot be explained, some people believe that they are miracles caused by God. There are many examples of <u>miracles</u> in religious texts (see p.9) and some people claim they still occur (miracles of <u>healing</u> at <u>Lourdes</u>, for example).

There are a variety of reasons why people believe in God
Religious revelation comes in many different forms. It can be as simple as reading an inspiring section of a holy book, or it can be a walking-on-water miracle — and everything in between.

Reasons for Belief: Miracles

Miracles are considered as important proof of God's existence and presence by many theists.

Miracles are described in the Scriptures

1) Christianity, Islam and Judaism all teach that at some points in history, some amazing and unexplainable things happened. These miracles are thought to be revelations of God.

2) The New Testament of the Bible describes many miracles. For example, Jesus feeding the 5000 (Mark 6), and Jesus walking on water (Mark 6).

3) Christians believe that Jesus performed miracles to show that he had God's power, and to demonstrate God's love for people who suffer.

4) There are many miraculous events described in the Jewish scriptures. Examples include G-d parting the Red Sea for Moses during the flight from Egypt (Exodus 14) and the fall of the walls of Jericho (Joshua 6).

Muslims believe that the Qur'an itself is a Miracle

1) Muslims believe the Qur'an is a miracle — the direct word of Allah, with a style that's impossible to copy.

2) Some Muslims believe that the Qur'an contains 'scientific miracles' — where facts discovered centuries later are described, such as the development of the human embryo.

> "Then We made the sperm-drop into a clinging clot, and We made the clot into a lump [of flesh], and We made [from] the lump, bones, and We covered the bones with flesh; then We developed him into another creation." Qur'an 23:14

Some people are Sceptical

1) Some non-religious people question whether these experiences are revelations of God at all.

2) They argue that they're just illusions brought on by religious hysteria or a desire to believe in something. Or that events that seem miraculous can actually be explained by science.

3) Some believers argue that miracles in religious texts should be interpreted symbolically rather than literally.

Religious texts include miracles
Christianity, Judaism and Islam all teach about miracles, but not everyone believes that they actually happened. Even some religious believers don't think they should be taken literally.

Questions

That's a pretty tricky section to be starting with. Have a crack at these questions.

Warm-up Questions

1) Describe the meaning of one type of truth.
2) Explain how it is possible to believe what both religion and science say about the origins of the world.
3) Name one theory which is an example of the design argument.
4) Give one reason why some people were upset by Darwin's theory of evolution.
5) Why might a person believe in God?

Practice Questions

Now try these slightly longer questions.

1) Draw lines to match each type of truth with the correct example.

    Aesthetic truth   Elizabeth I was a protestant queen.

    Historical truth   It's wrong to hurt others.

    Religious truth   God is everywhere.

    Moral truth   Copper conducts electricity.

    Scientific truth   Romeo and Juliet get married.

2) Copy and complete the passage below, choosing the correct words from the brackets.
    The **(cosmological / evolution)** argument states that everything in our Universe was caused by something else, so there must have been a **(creator / 'First Cause')** which prompted its creation.
    Religious people think that this 'First Cause' was **(Buddha / God)**. But the Big Bang theory suggests it was actually an **(explosion / earthquake)** which formed the Universe.
    Some **(atheists / religious people)** also believe in the Big Bang theory — they think God was responsible for **(evolution / the Big Bang)** and therefore the creation of the Universe.

3) Describe how religion can give people a reason for our lives on Earth.

4) Copy out and complete this passage, adding the correct words from the list below:
    Miracles   healing   scriptures   extraordinary   revelations   proof

    A miracle is an _____ event that cannot be explained — some people

    believe that they are caused by God. _____ are described in the Christian,

    Muslim and Jewish _____ — they are believed to be _____

    of God. Miracles are seen by many as _____ that God exists. Even today,

    people claim to have experienced miracles, like by _____ at Lourdes.

Section One — Summary Questions

Now you've had a bit of practice, have a go at these summary questions — they'll test what you've learnt from the whole of Section 1 — enjoy!

1) Describe the difference between a scientific truth and a religious truth.

2) Describe the difference between an atheist and an agnostic.

3) What does creationism mean?

4) Explain two interpretations of the story of creation in the Bible.

5) Explain the Muslim viewpoint on the scientific theories about creation.

6) What is the design argument?

7) Explain the Watchmaker Theory version of the design argument.

8) Give two reasons why someone might not accept the design argument.

9) Give two possible criticisms of the cosmological argument as proof of God's existence.

10) Explain how someone can believe in the Big Bang theory *and* the cosmological argument.

11) Explain how a person can believe in creation *and* the Big Bang theory.

12) Describe the theory of evolution.

13) How can Darwin's theory of evolution explain the existence of moral behaviour?

14) Which of the arguments in this section — the design, the cosmological or the evolution argument — do you think is most convincing? Why?

15) Explain the concept of stewardship.

16) Do you think religion helps to explain why we are here? Why? / Why not?

17) Give two different reasons why someone may believe in God.

18) Give an example of a numinous experience.

19) Give two other examples of revelation.

20) "It is not possible to prove God exists."
Discuss this statement, including different points of view, as well as your own viewpoint.
You should refer to a religion in your answer.

21) "The only reason people have religious faith is because of the way they were brought up."
Discuss this statement, including different points of view, as well as your own viewpoint.
You should refer to a religion in your answer.

Jesus

Christians believe that Jesus is the <u>Son of God</u> who lived on <u>Earth</u>.

Christians believe that **Jesus** is the **Son** of **God**

1) The angel <u>Gabriel</u> visited Mary to tell her she was going to have a son that she should call <u>Jesus</u> — he would be the <u>Son of God</u>. Jesus was born in a <u>stable</u> in Bethlehem.

2) Jesus's birth is celebrated at <u>Christmas</u> — an important Christian festival (see p.126).

3) The Bible says that even as a child, Jesus was filled with <u>wisdom</u>.

> "Everyone who heard him was amazed at his understanding and his answers." Luke 2:47 NIV

Jesus taught **Love** and **Forgiveness**

1) Jesus's message was one of <u>love</u>, <u>forgiveness</u> and <u>sincerity</u>.

2) It can be <u>difficult</u> to <u>love</u> and <u>forgive</u> people who have <u>hurt</u> you — but Jesus thought it was <u>important</u>.

3) Jesus was known as a <u>great teacher</u>. He told his followers about <u>God the Father</u> — a loving parent who would <u>provide</u> for them.

4) Jesus worked with the <u>poor</u>, the <u>disadvantaged</u> and those from <u>other communities</u> — his message was for <u>everyone</u>.

5) He taught that <u>anybody</u> can go to Heaven, as long as they have <u>faith</u> in God.

> "But I tell you, love your enemies and pray for those who persecute you," Matthew 5:44 NIV

Jesus had some **New Ideas**

1) Although he was a <u>Jew</u>, Jesus was also a <u>revolutionary</u> — he <u>acted differently</u> to what was expected of Jews at the time:

- He threw the <u>money changers</u> (people who traded currencies) out of the <u>Temple</u> because he thought what they were doing was <u>disrespectful</u> to God.
- He treated and spoke to <u>women</u> as <u>equals</u>.
- He <u>healed</u> people on the <u>Sabbath</u>, which is the Jewish day of rest.
- He once chose a <u>Samaritan</u> (who Jews traditionally disliked) as an example of a <u>good man</u> in a parable.

2) Eventually, after his death, Jesus's followers split from <u>Judaism</u> as a new religion — <u>Christianity</u>.

3) However, Christianity still has <u>a lot in common</u> with the religion it was <u>formed</u> from.

Jesus

Jesus had an enormous <u>impact</u> upon the <u>world</u> — and is not just remembered by Christians.

Jesus **Died** to **Forgive** the sins of **Humankind**

1) Christians believe that Jesus was <u>crucified</u> on the cross to <u>save</u> humankind from their <u>sins</u> (see p.137) — this is why Christians often wear a <u>cross</u>.

2) Although his tomb was guarded, his body <u>disappeared</u>. God raised him back to life — an event called the <u>resurrection</u>.

3) After his <u>resurrection</u>, Jesus was seen alive by over <u>500 people</u>.

4) Before he went to <u>Heaven</u>, he said he would <u>always</u> be with his followers, watching over them.

> Jesus's <u>death</u> and <u>resurrection</u> are still commemorated by Christians at <u>Easter</u> (see p.139).

Jesus is an **Important Figure** to people of **Different Religions**

1) In <u>Islam</u>, Jesus is one of the prophets, and the <u>Qur'an</u> includes many stories about Jesus.

2) Jesus inspired people to teach the importance of non-violence. The Hindu leader, <u>Mahatma Gandhi</u>, believed that Jesus was a <u>great teacher</u>.

> "...the highest example of one who wished to give everything, asking nothing in return, and not caring what creed might happen to be professed by the recipient."
> **Mahatma Gandhi**
> *The Modern Review, Oct. 1941*

3) Jesus lived <u>his life</u> in the way he taught others to live — his life is an <u>example</u> that people from a variety of religions try to <u>follow</u>.

Christians try to follow Jesus's Teachings

1) Although it's not always easy to <u>forgive</u> and to live <u>peacefully</u> and <u>selflessly</u>, Christians try to follow Jesus's example of how to live a <u>good life</u>.

2) Christians study the <u>Bible</u> to have a better understanding of how Jesus lived and what he taught about how they can change their lives to live more <u>like him</u>.

3) They believe that God will <u>forgive</u> their sins if they <u>repent</u> (regret their wrong actions and are truly sorry), thanks to Jesus's <u>sacrifice</u>.

4) Jesus left the '<u>Lord's Prayer</u>' as an important message to his followers (see p.51).

Jesus taught his followers to live with love and forgiveness

Christians believe Jesus was God's son. They believe he lived on Earth to teach them how to live, and to save them from their sins so that they can experience the best form of life.

Moses

Moses is important to Jews — he led them from <u>slavery</u> to the <u>Promised Land</u>.

Moses's mother **Hid** him to **Save** him

1) Moses was born in <u>Egypt</u> over a thousand years <u>before</u> the birth of Jesus.
2) When Moses was a baby, the <u>Jewish people</u> were <u>enslaved</u> in Egypt. The Egyptian Pharaoh feared that the Jews might rebel against him, so he ordered every Jewish baby boy to be <u>drowned</u>.
3) Moses's mother wanted to save him, so she <u>hid</u> him in a <u>basket</u> in the tall grasses of the river Nile.
4) The <u>Pharaoh's daughter</u> found him and <u>adopted</u> him, naming him <u>Moses</u>.

Moses led the Jews to Freedom

1) As an adult, Moses <u>didn't like</u> the way that the Jews were <u>treated</u> in Egypt.
2) One day, G-d spoke to Moses from a <u>burning bush</u> and told him to <u>free</u> the Jews and take them to the <u>Promised Land</u>.
3) Moses led the <u>Jews</u> out of Egypt — this is known as the <u>Exodus</u>. At one point, G-d gave Moses the power to <u>part</u> the <u>Red Sea</u> so they could <u>walk through</u> it.
4) At <u>Mount Sinai</u>, G-d gave Moses the <u>Torah</u> (see p.44-45) as part of a new <u>covenant</u> (deal). This was to replace the older covenant that G-d had made with <u>Abraham</u> (see p.81).
5) As the person who led the Jews from Egypt to the <u>Promised Land</u>, Moses is often seen as the founder of <u>Israel</u>.
6) Moses <u>died</u>, however, before he could enter Israel himself.

G-d gave Moses **Laws** for the Jews to **Live** by

1) The <u>Torah</u> which G-d gave to Moses on <u>Mount Sinai</u> included the <u>Ten Commandments</u>. It was detailed instructions on how to live a <u>good</u> and <u>holy</u> life.
2) Moses encouraged his followers to have <u>faith</u> that G-d would keep his word about the <u>Promised Land</u>, as long as they kept these commandments.
3) He taught the Jews that G-d was <u>all-powerful</u> and should be <u>loved</u> more than anyone or anything else.
4) Moses told the Jews not to pray to <u>idols</u>, and only to worship G-d.

Moses

Moses is still <u>important</u> to many different groups of people <u>today</u>.

Moses is a **Prophet** to **Jews**, **Muslims** and **Christians**

1) Moses is considered to be one of the most important <u>prophets</u> (someone who speaks God's message to humankind) in <u>Judaism</u>, <u>Islam</u> and <u>Christianity</u>.

2) Muslims call Moses <u>Musa</u>. In the <u>Qur'an</u>, he is mentioned more than any other person, and his life is described in <u>detail</u>.

3) Muslims see the Jewish <u>Exodus</u> from Egypt as very similar to the migration of <u>Muhammad and his followers</u> from Makkah (see p.113).

4) Moses is very important to <u>Jews</u> because he was the connection between <u>G-d</u> and the <u>Hebrews</u>.

Moses's **Actions** are **Remembered** today

1) The Jews' <u>escape from slavery</u> is a major event in Jewish history. Moses's actions are still remembered and celebrated during <u>Pesach</u> — the <u>Passover</u> festival (see p.61).

2) The Promised Land of <u>Israel</u> is still considered the most important place for Jews today. The <u>Temple</u> was built there, and Jews still make <u>pilgrimages</u> to visit its site.

3) The <u>Ten Commandments</u> have lasted over 3000 years and provide many of the <u>basic laws</u> for society to live by.

Moses passed G-d's word on to the Jewish people

Moses is important to members of the three main religions, and his life is recorded in detail in their holy scriptures. It's not surprising really — he had some pretty interesting experiences...

Muhammad

Muhammad was the <u>last</u>, and most important, <u>prophet</u> of Islam.

Muhammad was a **Descendant** of other **Prophets**

1) The Prophet Muhammad was born in <u>Makkah</u> (also known as 'Mecca') in Saudi Arabia in about <u>570 CE</u>.

2) He was descended from <u>Ishmael</u>, a son of <u>Abraham</u>, both of whom were prophets.

Muhammad was **Visited** by an **Angel**

1) Muhammad was a <u>spiritual</u> person who spent a lot of time <u>meditating</u>.

2) One day, he was visited by an <u>angel</u> while he was meditating. The angel told him to <u>recite</u>. The words that he recited are believed to be the words of <u>Allah</u> (God).

3) Muhammad received many other <u>revelations</u> during his life which he then <u>preached</u> to spread the word of Allah.

4) These recited words were eventually <u>written down</u> as the Qur'an.

Muhammad told **Muslims** what **Allah Wanted**

1) The Prophet Muhammad taught that <u>God is one</u> — meaning that nothing apart from <u>Allah</u> himself should be worshipped.

2) He said that <u>all</u> people from all backgrounds are <u>equally loved</u> by Allah.

3) Muhammad said that, to Allah, people with lots of good qualities are the most <u>honourable</u>. He also taught that the best people are those whose actions <u>help</u> all of <u>humanity</u>.

4) He preached that <u>vulnerable</u> people should be given extra <u>care</u>.

5) Muhammad also taught that <u>praying</u> five times a day, <u>fasting</u> during the month of Ramadan, making the <u>Hajj</u> pilgrimage and giving to <u>charity</u> are all very important (see p.33).

The **Sunnah** gives Muslims an **Example** of how to **Live**

1) Muhammad is the most important prophet for Muslims because they believe that he was the <u>last messenger</u> of God — he completed the <u>revelation</u> of Islam.

2) Muhammad's sayings, actions and recommendations are called the <u>Sunnah</u>. These rules of life can be found in the <u>Hadith</u>, which is the <u>second most important</u> text for Muslims, after the Qur'an.

Muhammad

Muhammad spread the word of <u>Islam</u>, which is one of the world's <u>biggest</u> religions.

Muslims' Lives are still Influenced by Muhammad

1) Muhammad was responsible for <u>spreading</u> the word of Allah and <u>establishing</u> Islam as a faith.

2) <u>Today</u>, Islam is one of the world's <u>largest</u> religions, so Muhammad's teachings still <u>influence</u> the lives of many people.

3) Muslims still fast during <u>Ramadan</u> (see p.62), go on pilgrimages to <u>Makkah</u> (see p.113) and <u>pray</u> five times a day (see p.53).

4) Muhammad's teachings about giving money to charity (<u>Zakat</u> — see p.33) have resulted in the creation of a number of Islamic charities, such as <u>Islamic Aid</u> and <u>Islamic Relief</u>.

Muhammad's Teachings are Preserved in the Qur'an

1) The <u>Qur'an</u> contains Muhammad's <u>revelations</u> — this means that Muslims feel <u>connected</u> to Muhammad when they study the Qur'an, and believe that his teachings will be taught <u>forever</u>.

2) <u>Arabic</u> has remained the common <u>language</u> of all Arab people, mainly because Muhammad's instructions in the <u>Qur'an</u> were written in Arabic.

Evidence of Muhammad's work is All Around us

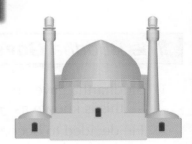

1) Muhammad built one of the world's first mosques — the <u>Al-Masjid al-Nabawi</u> in <u>Madinah</u>. Most mosques today are based on its design.

2) Muhammad was a <u>political leader</u> as well as a religious one — he contributed towards <u>conquests</u> of the time. The political development that he was involved with has helped to create the <u>world</u> as we see it today.

Muhammad was the last prophet of Islam

Allah spoke to Muhammad and Muhammad spoke to the people. He laid down the basis of the Islamic faith and is responsible for introducing many of the principal Islamic customs.

The Buddha

The Buddha was <u>born</u> as the <u>son</u> of an important <u>Indian leader</u>.

The **Buddha** had an **Extraordinary** birth

1) <u>Siddhartha Gautama</u> was born around the year <u>563 BCE</u> in Lumbini, in modern day <u>Nepal</u>. Siddhartha eventually became known as <u>the Buddha</u>.

2) Before he was born, Siddhartha's <u>mother</u>, Maya, had a <u>dream</u> in which a <u>white elephant</u> holding a <u>lotus flower</u> danced around her three times, and entered her womb through her side.

'The Buddha' is a <u>title</u> which means 'the enlightened one'.

3) The dream was <u>interpreted</u> by priests, who said that Maya was going to <u>give birth</u> to a <u>son</u> who would become either a <u>universal monarch</u> or a <u>buddha</u>.

4) When Siddhartha was <u>born</u>, a <u>sage</u> (wise man) named <u>Asita</u> examined Siddhartha's birthmarks and predicted that he would become a <u>buddha</u>.

Siddhartha's **Father** didn't tell him about **Suffering**

1) Siddhartha's <u>father</u> was a powerful <u>king</u> and Siddhartha spent his early life living in <u>palaces</u>.

2) His father tried to <u>protect</u> him from <u>suffering</u> by <u>not telling</u> him about <u>old age</u>, <u>sickness</u> or <u>death</u>.

3) However, at the age of <u>29</u>, Siddhartha finally went <u>outside the palace</u> and saw an <u>old man</u>. Soon afterwards he saw a <u>sick man</u>, then a <u>corpse</u>, then a <u>poor</u>, but <u>calm</u>, <u>monk</u>.

4) When Siddhartha realised that <u>suffering</u> existed, he decided to <u>give up</u> his position as a ruler and <u>go out</u> into the world to find the <u>truth</u> about coping with suffering.

The Buddha **Gave Up** a life of **Luxury** to search for the **Truth**

1) Siddhartha gave up all his <u>power</u>, <u>wealth</u> and sources of <u>pleasure</u> — this is known as '<u>The Great Renunciation</u>'.

2) He decided to become a <u>monk</u>. He hoped that this lifestyle might help him find the <u>meaning</u> of <u>suffering</u>.

3) He <u>studied meditation</u> under two holy men — but in the end he <u>didn't</u> believe either of them had the <u>answer</u>.

4) Next, Siddhartha tried to <u>give up</u> all <u>pleasures</u> completely. He ate so <u>little food</u> that he <u>nearly died</u>, and then realised that this was <u>not</u> the <u>answer</u> either.

5) One day he had a <u>vision</u>. He decided that it was best to take a <u>Middle Way</u> between living a life of luxury and giving up all pleasures.

The Buddha

The Buddha's teaching suggests a way of life for Buddhists to follow.

After following the **Middle Way**, the Buddha found **Enlightenment**

1) Siddhartha Gautama followed the Middle Way for several years. This meant taking a balanced approach to life, living in neither poverty nor luxury.

2) One day, while he was meditating under a tree, he finally achieved enlightenment.

3) To Buddhists, the term 'enlightenment' means 'awakening to the truth about life and the world'. Siddhartha was given the title 'The Buddha' once he had achieved enlightenment. This title means 'the one who is awake'.

4) Enlightenment means that the Buddha finally understood reality, overcame desire, and knew he was finally free from the cycle of rebirth — he had achieved nirvana.

Most Buddhists believe that when you die, you are reborn in another body again and again until you can escape the suffering of life by achieving enlightenment.

The Buddha spent the rest of his life **Teaching** his **Followers**

1) The Buddha spent the rest of his long life teaching the path to enlightenment.

2) According to Buddhist tradition, some of the Buddha's first teachings after achieving enlightenment were about the Four Noble Truths.

See p.109-110 for more about the Four Noble Truths.

3) The Four Noble Truths are about suffering and how to escape from it.

The **Noble Eightfold Path** is the **Fourth Noble Truth**

1) The Fourth Noble Truth teaches that escape from suffering is achieved by following the Noble Eightfold Path, also known as the Middle Way.

2) The Noble Eightfold Path is a list of eight different things that Buddhists should try to achieve, including doing and saying the right things — see p.110 for the full list.

3) The different steps on the path emphasise the importance of wisdom, meditation and doing what's right.

4) The path is often symbolised by the dharmachakra (see p.38) — a wheel which has eight spokes, each representing one step on the path.

Siddhartha Gautama wanted to find the meaning of life

The Buddha lived as a prince for the first 29 years of his life, unaware of all the suffering that existed in the world. After that, he set off on a spiritual journey to try to find the truth.

The Buddha

Buddhists follow the <u>precepts</u> as part of the Noble Eightfold Path in order to achieve <u>nirvana</u>.

A *Precept* is a *Rule* for living a *Good Life*

1) There are ten Buddhist precepts — <u>five main precepts</u> for <u>all</u> Buddhists to follow, and <u>five extra</u> for <u>monks and nuns</u>. They are based on the <u>Buddha's lifestyle</u>, which allowed him to achieve <u>enlightenment</u>.

2) These rules are believed to help Buddhists achieve <u>nirvana</u> — a state where they are <u>free</u> from <u>desire</u>, <u>suffering</u> and the cycle of <u>rebirth</u>.

Five precepts for all Buddhists:

1) Don't <u>harm</u> any <u>living thing</u>.
2) Don't <u>take</u> anything you were <u>not given</u>.
3) Don't have <u>sex</u> with anyone other than your <u>husband</u> or <u>wife</u>. <u>Monks</u> and <u>nuns</u> shouldn't have sex with <u>anyone</u>.
4) Don't <u>lie</u> or <u>gossip</u>.
5) Don't take <u>drugs</u> or drink <u>alcohol</u>.

Extra precepts for monks and nuns:

1) Don't <u>eat after midday</u>.
2) Don't <u>sing</u>, <u>dance</u> or <u>play music</u>.
3) Don't wear <u>jewellery</u> or <u>make-up</u>.
4) Don't <u>sleep</u> in a <u>luxurious bed</u>.
5) Don't <u>accept money</u>.

Buddhists *Today* still *Follow* the Buddha's *Teachings*

1) Buddhists try to <u>live</u> in a way which is in line with the Buddha's teachings, meaning that they must try to <u>think</u> and <u>act</u> in the <u>right way</u>.

2) They are careful about which <u>jobs</u> they take, as they can't do anything that might cause <u>danger</u> or <u>harm</u> to others, including jobs related to <u>alcohol</u>, <u>drugs</u> or <u>weapons</u>.

3) Buddhists believe in the laws of <u>karma</u> — if they do <u>good things</u> they will be <u>rewarded</u>, but if they <u>sin</u>, they'll be <u>punished</u>. This means that <u>helping</u> others and treating people <u>fairly</u> is really important.

4) Many Buddhists use <u>meditation</u> to help them — they believe that it's a good way to take <u>control</u> of their <u>own minds</u>, and to help ensure that their actions give them <u>good karma</u>.

5) Some forms of meditation help Buddhists to <u>calm</u> and <u>centre</u> their minds. Other forms encourage <u>kind thoughts</u> towards others.

Buddhists follow the precepts to try to achieve enlightenment

Most Buddhists try to follow the five main precepts, so many Buddhists are vegetarian and are careful about how they act. They try to act well so that they gain good karma.

Guru Nanak

The gurus were men who revealed Sikhism — Guru Nanak was the first of the ten gurus.

Guru Nanak was born a Hindu

1) Guru Nanak was the founder of Sikhism — he was born in the Punjab area of India in 1469 and died in 1539.
2) Nanak was brought up as a Hindu, and also learnt a lot about Islam, but he couldn't find spiritual peace.
3) When he was thirty, he disappeared for three days while bathing in a river.
4) Nanak returned and said that he had seen Heaven and heard God's voice. He said that God (Waheguru) had told him to teach others to rejoice in God's name.
5) It was this event that prompted him to preach what became the Sikh faith, becoming the first and most important guru.

Nanak wanted to bring Hindus and Muslims Together

1) After experiencing God, Nanak spent roughly the next 20 years making missionary journeys and teaching others about his insights. He established the first Sikh community in Kartarpur.
2) Nanak rejected the caste system which divided Hindus into different groups. He believed that everyone should be treated equally.
3) He spent a lot of time discussing religion with Hindus and Muslims, and he wanted to bring them together to help them see that they were all created by the same God, and were all looking for the same answers about life.
4) Nanak believed in following just one God, not worshipping a variety of deities.
5) Nanak criticised religious acts or rituals that he thought were empty or meaningless — he believed in truth and simplicity. Because of this, Sikhs don't do things like ritualistic yoga or have ordained priests.
6) Those who chose to follow Nanak became known as Sikhs (literally 'disciple' in Sanskrit).

The Guru's Followers Argued about what to do with his Body

1) When Nanak was about to die, the Hindus said they wanted to cremate him, and the Muslims said they wanted to bury him.
2) Guru Nanak told them to place flowers on both sides of his body — the Hindus would place them on his right and the Muslims on his left. He said that the side whose flowers were still fresh the next day could decide what happened to his body.
3) However, when the sheet that covered the Guru's dead body was lifted, all that remained were the two piles of flowers — both were still fresh. So, the Hindus cremated their pile, and the Muslims buried theirs.
4) This story emphasises the Guru's beliefs in equality and his respect for all religions.

Guru Nanak

Guru Nanak's <u>actions</u> and <u>beliefs</u> still affect how Sikhs live and worship <u>today</u>.

Guru Nanak's **Birth** is still **Celebrated Today**

1) Guru Nanak's <u>birthday</u> is usually celebrated in <u>November</u> — it is called <u>Guru Nanak Gurpurab</u>.
2) The <u>date</u> of the celebrations varies each year because it coincides with the <u>full moon</u>.
3) Guru Nanak's birthday is celebrated by reading the <u>Guru Granth Sahib</u> (the Sikh holy book — see p.48) from <u>beginning to end</u>. This is done by a group of Sikhs who take it in turns to read over a <u>48-hour</u> period which ends early on the Guru's birthday.
4) There are <u>processions</u> of <u>singers</u>, <u>musicians</u> and <u>dancers</u> during the day before his birthday.
5) Sikhs gather together to <u>sing</u>, <u>pray</u> and <u>eat</u> in the specially <u>decorated</u> gurdwara (see p.74-75).
6) Some followers of <u>other religions</u>, like Hindus, also celebrate the birth of the first guru because they respect his <u>philosophy</u> and <u>teachings</u>.

Guru Nanak believed that **Everyone** is **Equal** in God's eyes

1) <u>Equality</u> is still one of the main principles of Sikhism. It's symbolised in many aspects of Sikh worship — for example, the way that <u>everyone</u> sits on the floor of the gurdwara and is given the same amount of <u>karah parshad</u> (see p.75). This message had the greatest effect on the <u>poor</u>, and those at the <u>bottom of society</u>.
2) <u>Helping</u> those in need was another of the Guru's main <u>teachings</u>.
3) The Guru believed that <u>all</u> humans were capable of reaching <u>enlightenment</u> (becoming one with Waheguru) during their lifetime if they were <u>obedient</u> to God.
4) Nanak managed to bring many people <u>together</u> from different religions. He taught that there are no Hindus or Muslims, but only <u>God's people</u>.
5) Even today, followers of <u>any religion</u> are welcome to visit a <u>gurdwara</u> and eat together in the <u>langar</u> (see p.74).

Sikhs use the **Guru** as a **Role Model**

1) Guru Nanak's <u>teachings</u> are contained in the Guru Granth Sahib and form the <u>basis</u> of Sikhism.
2) He is considered a <u>role model</u>, whose ability to see <u>truth</u> is to be admired and followed.

The Guru was inspired by Hinduism and Islam to create Sikhism

There are many aspects of other religions, especially Hinduism, that can be seen in Sikhism. This is because the Guru grew up as a Hindu and was known for his respect of others' beliefs.

The Other Nine Gurus

After Guru Nanak, there were <u>nine</u> other human <u>gurus</u>.

Each *Guru Represents* a different *Divine Quality*

1) Guru Angad was the second guru. He began to <u>write down</u> Guru Nanak's teachings, and focused on teaching the Sikh faith to <u>children</u>. He represents <u>obedience</u>.

2) Guru Amar Das was concerned with <u>equality</u>. He fought against the <u>caste</u> system and the custom of <u>purdah</u>, which separated men and women in the temple.

3) Guru Ram Das began building the holy Sikh city of <u>Amritsar</u> (including the Golden Temple) and wrote the four main <u>verses</u> that are recited during Sikh <u>marriage ceremonies</u>. He represents <u>service</u>.

4) Guru Arjan is known for <u>self-sacrifice</u>. He collected the writings of the first four gurus, producing the first version of the Sikh scriptures — the <u>Adi Granth</u>. He died in captivity after being <u>arrested</u> for using Muslim references in the Sikh scriptures.

5) Guru Har Gobind was the sixth guru. He led the Sikhs to <u>fight</u> against the Mughals who ruled over them at the time. He's known for <u>justice</u>.

6) The seventh guru, Har Rai, was a <u>peaceful</u> man who dedicated his time to setting up free medical help for those who needed it. He represents <u>mercy</u>.

Guru Nanak, the first guru, represents humility.

7) Guru Har Krishan became leader when he was <u>five</u>, and died aged eight of smallpox. He represents <u>purity</u> because he spent most of his time <u>caring for others</u>, regardless of their background.

8) Guru Tegh Bahadur represents <u>tranquillity</u>. He protected the <u>freedom of religion</u> in India.

9) The <u>final</u> human guru was Gobind Singh, who represents <u>royal courage</u>. He founded the <u>Khalsa</u> — the community of the pure. He told every Sikh man to add the word "Singh" (<u>lion</u>) to his name, because they should be as <u>brave</u> as lions. Sikh women added "<u>Kaur</u>" (princess) to their names because the guru said that they should be treated with <u>respect</u>.

10) After the death of Guru Gobind Singh, the <u>Adi Granth</u> became the final guru. The Adi Granth (known as the <u>Guru Granth Sahib</u> today) is the word of the Guru, so it is <u>treated</u> as if it were a living guru (see p.48).

The *Gurus* were *God's Messengers*

1) The gurus are believed to have been <u>perfect</u> — they weren't <u>reborn</u> because of the law of <u>karma</u>, but because God wanted them to be his <u>messengers</u>. God used them to <u>reveal</u> himself to the people.

2) This is why the gurus were so <u>intelligent</u> and <u>wise</u>, even when they were young — they had nothing left to <u>learn</u> when they were born.

3) But Sikhs do not <u>worship</u> the gurus — they only worship <u>God</u>.

The Guru Granth Sahib is the only remaining guru

The gurus were enlightened men (or boys) who all worked to pass on God's message about Sikhism. Once this message was written in the scriptures, a human guru wasn't necessary.

24

Vyasa

Vyasa was an important Hindu leader and teacher.

Vyasa chose to study the Scriptures at a Young Age

1) According to legend, Vyasa's parents were Parashara, a religious wise-man, and Satyavati. It is said that Parashara had previously predicted a date when the greatest man of our age would be born — this was when Vyasa was born.

2) At a very young age, Vyasa told his parents that he wanted to live in the forests to learn from the gurus. This was where he learnt the Vedas (the most ancient and sacred of the Hindu scriptures).

Vyasa wanted Everyone to be able to access Hindu Teachings

1) After learning the Vedas, Vyasa became a teacher and a priest. He gathered a group of followers to spread his ideas across India.

2) Vyasa wanted to help people understand the ancient teachings of Hinduism and see their relevance, so he divided the Vedas into four parts to make it easier to understand.

3) It's believed that Vyasa wrote or collected the Mahabharata — a collection of epic poetry that teaches truths about the gods and the way we should live. He believed that this would make Hindu teachings easier for the common people to understand.

4) Tradition says that Ganesha, the elephant god, said he would help him write the Mahabharata down as long as Vyasa did not pause while telling the story.

5) These writings helped to explain and develop Hinduism, which was Vyasa's task from the gods.

The name Vyasa means "split" — Vyasa split the Vedas into four sections to make them more accessible.

Hindus believe that Vyasa Never Died

1) Many Hindus believe that Vyasa is an avatar of Vishnu (a human version of the god Vishnu — the sustaining god of the Universe).

2) Hindus also believe that Vyasa is a Chiranjivi — one of the seven immortal people who have never died. He is said to roam the Earth for the well-being of everyone.

Vyasa

Even though he lived thousands of years ago, many of the ideas that Vyasa taught his followers through his scriptures are key to the way Hindus live today.

Guru Purnima celebrates Vyasa's birthday

1) Vyasa was given the title "Guru" because he had a great knowledge of the religious scriptures, he was said to be blessed by the gods, and he worked selflessly to pass on his knowledge to others.

2) Vyasa also showed a great deal of compassion and encouraged others to do so. Hindus are influenced by Vyasa — they try to be truthful and compassionate too.

3) Hindus remember Vyasa and celebrate his birthday with a festival called Guru Purnima.

4) Guru Purnima takes place on the day of a full moon during July or August. Hindus perform a puja (act of worship) and often spend the whole day praying and meditating.

5) The festival is often the beginning of a time focused on religious learning — believers try to think about some of the scriptures that Vyasa wrote. Hindus believe that following the teachings of the gurus is the best way to worship them.

The laws of Karma were present in the Mahabharata

1) Most of Vyasa's teachings can be found in the Mahabharata — they form part of the story and the dialogues between the key characters.

2) The Mahabharata teaches the laws of karma. Karma states that all actions have consequences.

3) It encourages Hindus to live a good life while in human form on Earth — seeking to complete their dharma (duty).

4) Living well and fulfilling their duty pleases the gods, and earns Hindus good karma — eventually resulting in moksha (union with Brahman, God).

5) The principles of dharma, karma and moksha are shown in the Mahabharata through the characters' relationships — especially their family relationships. For example, King Dhritarashtra chose to ignore his sons' faults, and this eventually led to his family's downfall.

Vyasa wanted to make the Hindu scriptures more accessible

You might notice some similarities between the different religious figures in this section. For one thing, they all spent a lot of time helping others — particularly in a spiritual sense.

Questions

You need to remember the key points about all the religious figures in this section.

Warm-up Questions

1) Describe one of Jesus's main teachings.
2) Name the Jewish festival that celebrates the Jews' escape from Egypt.
3) Explain why Muhammad is the most important prophet for Muslims.
4) Why did the Buddha give up his life of luxury?
5) Which Sikh guru is known for self-sacrifice?

Practice Questions

Now you've got started, try these slightly longer questions.

1) Draw lines to match each religious figure with the correct religion.

   Vyasa   Judaism

   Muhammad   Islam

   Moses   Sikhism

   Guru Nanak   Hinduism

2) Copy out and complete these sentences, adding the correct words from the list below:

   freedom   Moses   Jewish   laws   societies

   a) Moses was a _____ man, but he is recognised as a Jewish, Christian and Muslim prophet.

   b) G-d asked Moses to lead the Jews to _____ from slavery in Egypt.

   c) While _____ was travelling to the Promised Land, G-d gave him some _____ which include the Ten Commandments.

   d) Most _____ in the world today have laws which are similar to some of The Ten Commandments — they're still relevant, even after thousands of years.

3) Name three of the five precepts that all Buddhists should follow.

4) Are these statements about Guru Nanak true or false?

   a) Guru Nanak was the founder of Hinduism.

   b) He rejected the Hindu caste system.

   c) He tried to bring people from different religions together.

   d) His followers perform many complicated rituals.

5) Why did Vyasa write the Mahabharata? Do you think it is useful to Hindus?

Section Two — Summary Questions

Give these questions a go to see how much you've learnt. If you get stuck, all of the answers can be found in this section — so take another look until you're feeling confident.

1) How did Jesus describe God?

2) List three ways in which Jesus was a revolutionary.

3) Explain why the story of Jesus's death is important to Christians.

4) Give an example of how Jesus has influenced people of religions other than Christianity.

5) Why did Moses's mother hide him?

6) Explain why Moses is important to Jews.

7) What is the Sunnah?

8) Describe two ways in which Muhammad's teachings still affect the lives of Muslims today.

9) In what way do Muslims believe that Muhammad's teachings will be taught forever?

10) Explain what is meant by 'the Middle Way' in Buddhism.

11) What is the purpose of the ten precepts in Buddhism?

12) How do the Buddha's teachings affect how Buddhists live their lives today?

13) Why is Guru Nanak important to Sikhs?

14) Describe what happened to Guru Nanak's body after he died, and explain what this symbolises for Sikhs.

15) Explain why male Sikhs often have 'Singh' in their name, and female Sikhs often have 'Kaur' in their name.

16) What was the name of the last human Sikh guru?

17) Why isn't there a human Sikh guru today?

18) How was Vyasa's birth and childhood special?

19) How do Hindus celebrate Vyasa's birthday?

20) Why did Vyasa choose to write about characters' relationships in the Mahabharata?

21) "Religious figures play a key role in helping believers decide how to live their lives." Discuss this statement, including different points of view, as well as your own viewpoint. You should refer to at least one religion in your answer.

22) "Religious figures can only be a source of inspiration to followers of their own religion." Discuss this statement, including different points of view, as well as your own viewpoint. You should refer to at least one religion in your answer.

23) Do you think that it's possible to follow the examples of religious leaders such as Jesus or Muhammad in modern-day life? Why? / Why not?

The Nature of God and Religion

Almost all religions believe in one or more <u>supernatural beings</u>, known as <u>gods</u>.

A *God* is a Supernatural Being

1) In most religions, a god is a <u>supernatural being</u> who <u>created</u> the world and the Universe.

2) A god is also often seen as being the <u>ruler</u> of the Universe and a <u>moral guide</u>.

3) In some religions, a god is a <u>being</u> or <u>spirit</u> that has <u>power</u> over an aspect of <u>nature</u> or <u>human life</u>.

What's God Like? — *The debate continues...*

1) For thousands of years, religious thinkers have tried to work out <u>what God is like</u>.

2) There are three main issues that are debated:

1) Is God a '*Person*' or a '*Force*'?

Personal god

1) God is seen as a 'person', but a <u>divine</u> (supernatural) and almighty person. If God is personal, then a relationship is possible through <u>prayer</u> — which can be a '<u>conversation</u>' with God.

2) However, if God is personal, then it seems difficult for them to be <u>omnipresent</u> (everywhere at once).

Impersonal god

1) God is seen as a kind of <u>force</u>.

2) However, it is very <u>difficult</u> to have a <u>relationship</u> with a force.

2) *Where* is God?

1) An <u>immanent</u> god is <u>present</u> in the world, and takes an <u>active role</u> in humanity.

2) However, it is hard to understand why an immanent god does not <u>always intervene</u> to sort out <u>evil</u> and <u>suffering</u>.

3) A <u>transcendent</u> god is <u>separate</u> from the world and <u>doesn't interfere</u> in human history.

4) This view can make God seem <u>remote</u> and <u>distant</u> from our life on Earth.

5) Lots of religious believers believe that God is a <u>blend</u> of both immanent and transcendent.

It's very difficult to work out what God's like

Religious believers have wondered and debated for centuries about what God is like, and this page covers two of the main questions. The next page has one more big question for you.

The Nature of God and Religion

Here's another page exploring some of the big issues about <u>God</u> and <u>religion</u>.

3) How Many Gods are there?

1) <u>Monotheism</u> is the belief in <u>one god</u>.
   Jews, Christians, Muslims and
   Sikhs all believe in one god.

2) <u>Polytheism</u> is the belief in <u>more than one god</u>,
   e.g. ancient Greek and Roman religions,
   and some forms of Hinduism.

> Christianity is a monotheistic religion, but Christians believe that God is actually <u>three parts in one</u>, known as the <u>Trinity</u>. This is covered in detail on p.31.

Religions are made up of people who believe in the Same God

1) A religion is a <u>system of beliefs</u> about a god or gods.

2) Religions are made up of <u>people</u> who believe the <u>same things</u> about the god or gods that the religion is based on.

3) All of the world's major religions have been around for hundreds, if not <u>thousands of years</u>. However, many religions are divided into <u>subgroups</u> believing slightly different things. In Christianity, these subgroups are called <u>denominations</u>.

> Roman Catholic, Orthodox, Methodist and Anglican are all Christian <u>denominations</u>.

Religion is important to All Societies

1) Although <u>religions</u> might only seem relevant to the people who <u>practise</u> them, they form an important part of all <u>societies</u>.

2) Religion can play a role in the lives of nonbelievers, particularly in bringing people and <u>communities together</u> for <u>festivals</u>, e.g. Diwali, Christmas and Hanukkah.

3) Lots of <u>charities</u> (e.g. Christian Aid and Islamic Aid) are run by religious groups, or by people inspired to do something good because of their <u>faith</u>.

4) Religion provides believers with <u>guidance</u> on how they should behave. It can make people more likely to live <u>moral</u> lives and obey the <u>law</u>.

There are no clear answers to any of these questions...

...but I reckon the world would be a pretty boring place without a bit of mystery. The next few pages explore lots more about what different religions believe about God, so let's get going...

Beliefs About God

Christians and Jews believe in <u>one God</u>, who they believe <u>created</u> the <u>whole Universe</u>.

Judaism and Christianity say Similar things about God...

1) <u>Christianity</u> grew <u>directly from Judaism</u> (Jesus was Jewish) and so the two religions <u>share</u> a <u>basic concept</u> of God.
2) <u>Both faiths</u> see God as <u>omnipotent</u> (all-powerful), <u>omnipresent</u> (everywhere) and <u>omniscient</u> (all-knowing).
3) They also believe that God is <u>perfect</u> and has given humans <u>free will</u>.

...but there are some Key Differences

1) The <u>biggest difference</u> is the <u>Christian belief</u> in the <u>Trinity</u> (see p.31) — Jews <u>don't believe</u> that <u>Jesus</u> was the <u>Son of God</u>.
2) Christians don't share the <u>Jewish belief</u> that <u>pictures</u> of God should never be <u>drawn</u>.

Jews Believe that G-d is...

...ONE — Jews believe there is only <u>one G-d</u>.

...A PERSON — G-d is not an abstract 'force'. Human beings were made in the <u>image of G-d</u> (though this doesn't mean G-d looks like us).

...THE CREATOR — G-d created the Universe and everyone in it. Jews believe that <u>creation</u> makes it <u>obvious</u> that G-d <u>exists</u>.

...THE SUSTAINER — G-d didn't just create the Universe and then abandon it. Rather, his <u>energy</u> keeps it going.

...HOLY — '<u>Holy</u>' means '<u>set apart</u>' or '<u>completely pure</u>'.

...OMNIPOTENT — 'Omnipotent' means '<u>all-powerful</u>'.

...OMNISCIENT — G-d <u>knows everything</u>, including people's thoughts, secrets and dreams.

...OMNIPRESENT — G-d is present throughout the <u>whole Universe</u>.

...THE LAWGIVER — Jews see the <u>Torah</u> as <u>G-d's laws</u> for humankind.

...THE TRUE JUDGE — Jews believe they will all <u>face G-d</u> one day to be judged on whether they have lived <u>good</u> or <u>bad</u> lives.

...THE REDEEMER — Jews believe G-d is <u>merciful</u>. He will <u>save</u> people from sin and suffering.

Jews and Christians believe different things about Jesus

Judaism and Christianity share a number of beliefs about God. However, Jesus is seen as another prophet for Jews, whereas Christians believe that he is the Son of God.

Beliefs About God

The key difference between Jewish and Christian beliefs about God is that Christians believe that the one God has three persons — the Father, the Son (Jesus) and the Holy Spirit.

Christians believe in *The Trinity* — the *Father...*

1) For many Christians, God the Father is the God of the Old Testament.

2) In the first chapter of the Bible, Genesis 1, God is described as the Creator of heaven and earth.

> "In the beginning God created the heavens and the earth."
> Genesis 1:1 NIV

3) Seeing God as the Creator is important to Christians — they believe that it means the world must be good if it was created by a good God.

4) The term 'Father' is a title of respect for God, and is used by Jesus: "...when you pray... pray to your Father, who is unseen." (Matthew 6:6 NIV).

...the Son...

1) Christians believe that Jesus is the incarnation (human form) of God.

2) They believe that God sent Jesus, his son, to Earth to show how much he loves us.

3) For Christians, Jesus is the Christ or Messiah ('anointed one') promised by God and prophesied by Isaiah in the Old Testament.

4) Jesus's life provides a model for Christian behaviour and obedience to God.

> JESUS OFFERS CHRISTIANS SALVATION FROM SIN
> Christians believe that through Jesus's death, he won forgiveness for the sins of all people. Jesus lived a perfect life (without sin), but God placed the sins of the world on him at his crucifixion. Christians believe that Christ's victory over sin and death was revealed in his resurrection (see p.137-138).

...and the Holy Spirit

1) Christians believe that the Holy Spirit is the presence of God in the world.

2) Some believe that the Holy Spirit guides them personally in being good Christians.

3) Charismatic Christians believe that the Holy Spirit can descend on them during worship, giving them a variety of gifts, such as speaking in tongues (unknown languages).

4) Christians believe that the Holy Spirit guides the Church and influences history for good.

The Trinity is three persons in one God

The Trinity has been studied, debated and discussed for hundreds of years, but it shouldn't take you that long to learn this page. Just remember that Christians believe the Trinity is one God.

Beliefs About Allah

Islam shares a lot of <u>history</u> and <u>beliefs</u> with Judaism and Christianity. But Muslims believe Islam is the '<u>final word of God</u>'.

The **Muslim** name for God is **Allah**

'Allah' written in Arabic.

1) Muslims call God '<u>Allah</u>'. Allah is the Arabic word for 'God'.
2) '<u>Islam</u>' means '<u>submission</u>' or '<u>surrender</u>' to Allah.
3) According to Islamic teaching, Allah is the <u>creator</u> of everything.
4) There are <u>ninety-nine names</u> for Allah in the Qur'an. Each one tells you something about what Muslims believe about Allah.

> The names for Allah include: <u>Ar-Khaliq</u> — The <u>Creator</u>; <u>Ar-Rahman</u> — The <u>Compassionate</u>; and <u>Al-Aziz</u> — The <u>Almighty</u>. Allah is also called The <u>Provider</u>, The <u>Just</u>, The <u>Maintainer</u>, The <u>Hearer</u> and The <u>Real Truth</u>.

"He is **Allah**, the **One**, Allah is **Eternal** and **Absolute**"

1) The quotation above is taken from surah (chapter) 112 of the Qur'an. It describes the <u>basic principle</u> that <u>Allah is one</u>.
2) This belief in the <u>oneness</u> of Allah is a very important principle of Islam, and is known as <u>Tawhid</u>.
3) Muslims believe Allah <u>cannot</u> be thought of in human terms — he is the <u>Supreme Being</u> and has <u>no equal</u>.
4) Muslims also believe that their lives are <u>predestined</u> (determined in advance) by <u>Allah</u> — but they still believe that everyone has <u>free will</u>.
5) Allah is considered to be both <u>transcendent</u> and <u>immanent</u> (see p.28):

Transcendent

Muslims believe Allah is the <u>creator</u> of the Universe, but is <u>outside</u> and <u>beyond</u> both <u>space</u> and <u>time</u>. He has <u>always</u> existed.

Immanent

The Qur'an says: "And We have already created man and <u>know</u> what his soul whispers to him, and We are <u>closer</u> to him than [his] <u>jugular vein</u>." <u>Qur'an 50:16</u>. (In this passage 'We' refers to Allah and 'him' or 'his' refers to humankind.)

Muslims believe in one God — Allah

There are ninety-nine names for Allah in the Qur'an, but there wouldn't have been room for anything else if we'd put them all on this page. Head to the next page for more about Allah.

Beliefs About Allah

Muslims strive to learn the Qur'an and get to know Allah as much as they can.

Allah gave his Message to the Prophets

1) The message of Allah was delivered by the prophets. The Qur'an mentions 25 prophets, including Musa (Moses) and Isa (Jesus).

2) The last of the prophets was the Prophet Muhammad (see p.16-17), who brought Allah's message to the people.

3) Muslims believe that the Qur'an is the word of Allah. Many Muslims learn it by heart, and all try to live according to the guidelines found in it.

4) Muslims believe that Allah is good and kind. However, there is a belief in a devil (called Iblis or Shaytan) who was cast out by Allah and tries to lead people away from him.

5) Some Muslims think that Allah allows Shaytan to use this power to test and tempt believers — they have the free will to resist.

There are Five main ways to Know Allah

The Five Pillars of Islam provide opportunities to know and be close to Allah. They are:

1 Shahadah

A statement of belief which is recited. It says that Allah is the only God and that Muhammad is his messenger.

2 Salat

Praying to Allah five times a day (see p.53).

Muslims praying.

3 Zakat

Giving money to charity to help the poor and those in need.

4 Sawm

Fasting during the month of Ramadan (see p.62).

5 Hajj

A pilgrimage to the holy city of Makkah (see p.113) which Muslims must try to complete at least once in their lives.

The Five Pillars of Islam help Muslims to know Allah

The Qur'an and the Five Pillars of Islam exist so that Muslims can become closer to Allah and get to know him better. Muslims believe Jesus was a prophet but not the Son of God.

Beliefs About Waheguru

Sikhism is a monotheistic religion — Sikhs believe in and worship one God.

Sikhs believe in One God

1) Sikhs believe there is only one God, who has many qualities and names but only one form.
2) Sikhs believe that all monotheistic religions are following the same God.
3) Sikhs believe that it is wrong to worship any statues or idols.

Sikhs have Different Names for God

1) Sikhs use several names for God, but believe that none of them can suitably describe God.

- Waheguru means 'Wonderful Lord'. It is the most common name used by Sikhs to refer to God.
- Sat Nam means 'True Name'. It shows that God is the truth.
- Akal Purakh means 'Eternal One' — God is an eternal being responsible for creating everything and everyone.

2) Sikhs believe that God is both immanent (present in the world) and transcendent (separate from the world), is available to everyone and has created all humans equal.
3) Waheguru has no human form and instead lives in the hearts of humans.

The Mool Mantar describes Waheguru

1) The Mool Mantar is found at the beginning of each section of the Guru Granth Sahib. It is a list of the most important qualities of Waheguru and forms the basis of the Sikh faith.
2) Sikhs believe that the Mool Mantar was spoken by Guru Nanak when he reached the state of enlightenment.
3) Every new Sikh must learn it by heart, and many meditate on it every morning.
4) The Mool Mantar teaches that there is only one God.
5) Sikhs believe that God is immortal, without fear or hate, and that God is the creator.

Waheguru is the name most often used by Sikhs for God

Sikhs spend a lot of time meditating on the names and the qualities of God. The Mool Mantar is one of the most important parts of the Guru Granth Sahib as it helps them to do this.

Hindu and Buddhist Beliefs About Gods

Hindus and Buddhists have very <u>different views</u> about God.

Hindus believe in *One Supreme God* who has *Many Forms*

1) Hindus believe that there is <u>one supreme God</u>, called <u>Brahman</u>. Brahman is <u>eternal</u>, <u>omnipresent</u> and the <u>creator</u> of everything.

2) There are <u>three</u> main aspects of Brahman: <u>Brahma</u>, the <u>creator</u>; <u>Vishnu</u>, the <u>preserver</u>; and <u>Shiva</u>, the <u>destroyer</u>. These three gods together are known as the <u>Trimurti</u>.

3) There are <u>hundreds</u> of other Hindu <u>deities</u> (gods and goddesses), which all represent <u>different aspects</u> of Brahman. Important examples are <u>Krishna</u>, <u>Indra</u> and <u>Mahadevi</u>.

4) Hindus <u>pray</u> to these deities instead of praying <u>directly</u> to Brahman.

5) <u>Krishna</u> is an <u>avatar</u> of <u>Vishnu</u>. An avatar is an <u>incarnation</u> of a god that appears on <u>Earth</u> in human or animal form. Hindus believe that avatars help <u>spread goodness</u> and <u>reduce evil</u>.

6) Having a <u>personal relationship</u> with a god is <u>not</u> part of Hinduism, and a person's <u>actions</u> are considered more important than their <u>beliefs</u>.

Brahman *Lives* in *Everyone*

1) Hindus believe that there's a <u>part of Brahman</u> in the <u>atman</u> (spirit or soul) of every living thing.

2) Hindus believe that the atman goes through <u>repeated cycles of birth and death</u>, known as <u>reincarnation</u> (see p.91).

Buddhists *Don't Believe* in a *Creator* god

1) Buddhists <u>don't</u> believe in a <u>creator god</u> in the same way that believers from most other major religions do.

2) Buddhism is about <u>personal development</u> rather than interacting with a god or gods. This development includes <u>meditating</u>, gaining <u>wisdom</u> and becoming more <u>moral</u>.

3) This helps Buddhists move along the path towards <u>enlightenment</u>, where there is <u>no more suffering</u>.

4) The <u>Buddha</u> was <u>not</u> a god and Buddhists don't worship him. However, they do <u>respect</u> him and believe that following his <u>teachings</u> will help them on the path to <u>enlightenment</u>.

5) Buddhists do believe in gods, as spirits, which live in a <u>different world</u> to us (see p.91).

Hindus have many gods, but Buddhists don't think gods are important

Hindus believe in one supreme God, known as Brahman, but worship hundreds of different forms of Brahman. Buddhists see the Buddha as an important man, but not a god.

The Significance of Religious Symbols

Religious believers use <u>symbols</u> to remind them of their <u>faith</u> and their <u>God</u>.

The **Cross** is an important **Christian** symbol

1) The <u>cross</u> is the most commonly used symbol of the <u>Christian faith</u>.
2) It reminds Christians that <u>Jesus died on the cross</u> to <u>save</u> them from their <u>sins</u>, but also that he <u>rose again</u> after his death (see p.137).
3) Many Christians wear a cross on a <u>necklace</u> as a symbol of their <u>faith</u>.
4) A <u>crucifix</u> is a cross which has a <u>figure of Jesus</u> on it. These are most commonly found in <u>Catholic</u> and <u>Orthodox</u> churches and are also <u>worn</u> by worshippers of those denominations.

Early Christians used the **Ichthus** as their symbol

1) <u>Ichthus</u> is a word that means <u>fish</u> in <u>Greek</u>. The Greek word for fish was used as an <u>acronym</u> for 'Jesus Christ, God's Son, Saviour', so the symbol is sometimes known as the 'Jesus fish'.
2) It was used as a kind of <u>secret code</u> by early Christians — one Christian would trace <u>half</u> of the symbol in the <u>dust</u> on the ground and would wait to see if <u>someone else completed</u> it. If they did, then they were most likely a Christian.
3) Christians did this because their religion was <u>forbidden</u> by the <u>Roman government</u> and so they had to meet in <u>secret</u>.
4) Some Christians still use the ichthus on <u>jewellery</u> or <u>car stickers</u> to show they're Christians.

The **Star of David** is a symbol of **Judaism**

1) The Star of David is a symbol made up of <u>two equilateral triangles</u> placed together.
2) It is also called the <u>Magen David</u> (Shield of David), which refers to a <u>Jewish</u> <u>legend</u> where King David's <u>shield</u> helped him <u>win</u> an <u>intense battle</u>.
3) The star <u>reminds</u> Jews that <u>G-d</u> is their <u>protector</u>, just as he protected David.
4) The symbol has been adopted by Jews as a symbol of their <u>faith</u>, and is found on the outside of <u>synagogues</u> and on Jewish <u>tombstones</u>.
5) When <u>Israel</u> was founded as a Jewish state, the Star of David was given more <u>significance</u> by being included on the Israeli <u>flag</u>.

The cross and the Star of David are widely used symbols

Christians around the world use the cross as a symbol of their faith, just as lots of Jews use the Star of David as a symbol. Early Christians primarily used the ichthus rather than the cross.

The Significance of Religious Symbols

Symbols have <u>different</u> amounts of <u>importance</u> for <u>Muslims</u> and <u>Hindus</u>.

The **Star and Crescent** has become a symbol of **Islam**

1) The <u>star</u> and <u>crescent</u> is used by some Muslims as a symbol of their religion.

2) The symbol was used by the Muslim <u>Ottoman Empire</u> and was adopted as a symbol of the <u>Muslim faith</u> during the <u>twentieth century</u>.

3) Lots of <u>Muslim countries</u> including <u>Pakistan</u>, <u>Turkey</u> and <u>Tunisia</u> use the symbol on their national <u>flags</u>.

4) Some Muslims <u>refuse</u> to use the star and crescent because the symbol was <u>not originally</u> a <u>Muslim</u> symbol and has only been adopted recently.

'Om' is a **Sacred** symbol for **Hindus**

1) '<u>Om</u>' is the <u>Hindu</u> symbol for <u>Brahman</u> (God). Hindus believe that it is <u>impossible</u> to fully <u>describe</u> <u>Brahman</u> using words, and so use the <u>symbol</u> instead.

2) The symbol is considered to be the most <u>sacred</u> symbol in Hinduism. It is found on <u>shrines</u>, worn on <u>pendants</u>, and is often included on <u>letterheads</u>.

3) The number <u>three</u> is an important part of the symbol as it symbolises the three main aspects of Brahman — <u>creator</u>, <u>preserver</u> and <u>destroyer</u> (see p.35).

The 'Om' symbol has a **Sound**

1) According to Hindu <u>scriptures</u>, 'Om' is the <u>sound</u> that was <u>present</u> at the start of the <u>creation</u> of the Universe. It <u>represents</u> the past, present and future.

2) Lots of Hindus spend time <u>chanting</u> the word 'Om', which they believe will fill them with a new <u>strength</u> and help them to <u>remove distractions</u> when trying to <u>focus</u> on <u>Brahman</u>.

3) 'Om' is also said at the <u>start of the day</u> and at the beginning of <u>journeys</u>.

'Om' represents Brahman in Hinduism

The star and crescent has become a recognisable symbol for Muslims and Islamic communities or countries. 'Om' is a symbol which is sacred to Hindus and is used in worship and daily life.

The Significance of Religious Symbols

The dharmachakra and khanda represent <u>important beliefs</u> for <u>Buddhists</u> and <u>Sikhs</u>.

The **Dharmachakra** *is an important symbol in* **Buddhism**

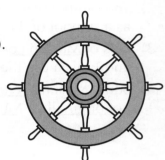

1) The <u>dharmachakra</u> (Wheel of Law) represents the <u>teachings</u> of <u>the Buddha</u> and the <u>law</u> (dharma) that he spoke about.

2) There are usually <u>eight spokes</u> on the wheel, representing the <u>Noble Eightfold Path</u> that the Buddha taught Buddhists to follow (see p.110).

3) The <u>rim</u> around the spokes is a reminder for some Buddhists of the <u>concentration</u> that's <u>required</u> in order to <u>stay</u> on the <u>path</u>.

4) The '<u>hub</u>' at the centre of the wheel represents <u>moral discipline</u>.

5) The wheel also symbolises the <u>cycle</u> of <u>life</u>, <u>death</u> and <u>rebirth</u> which Buddhists believe humans experience until they reach the state of <u>enlightenment</u> (see p.110).

6) The wheel has become a widespread <u>symbol</u> in <u>Buddhism</u> and is found in lots of Buddhist <u>art</u>.

The **Khanda** *is the symbol of* **Sikhism**

1) The <u>khanda</u> is the most important Sikh symbol and <u>reflects</u> some of the most important <u>aspects</u> of the Sikh <u>religion</u>.

2) The khanda appears on the <u>Nishan Sahib</u> (the Sikh holy flag) that flies outside every <u>gurdwara</u>. It is also frequently used in Sikh <u>decorations</u> in the gurdwara and the home.

3) There are <u>three</u> distinct parts of the khanda:

① A solid circle (chakra)

The <u>chakra</u> symbolises the fact that there is <u>one God</u> who is <u>perfect</u> and <u>doesn't</u> have a <u>beginning</u> or an <u>end</u>.

② A double-edged sword (khanda)

The single <u>double-edged sword</u> at the centre of the symbol represents <u>divine knowledge</u>, with <u>sharp edges</u> to separate <u>truth</u> from <u>falsehood</u>.

③ Two interlocking swords (kirpans)

The <u>two kirpans</u> symbolise <u>spiritual</u> and <u>political</u> power. They remind Sikhs of their <u>responsibilities</u> to <u>society</u>, as well as to their <u>faith</u>.

The khanda reminds Sikhs of God and their responsibilities

The dharmachakra symbolises lots of different things that Buddhists believe and follow. The khanda is made up of three separate parts which all represent something specific to Sikhs.

Sikhism and the Five Ks

The Five Ks are <u>physical objects</u> that remind <u>Sikhs</u> of important aspects of their <u>faith</u>.

Sikhs have *Five Physical Symbols* of faith

1) The <u>Five Ks</u> are things that must be <u>worn</u> at <u>all times</u> by devoted Sikhs called the <u>Khalsa</u>. Each item <u>represents</u> or <u>symbolises</u> something <u>different</u>.
2) This custom was started by <u>Guru Gobind Singh</u>, who wanted Sikhs to <u>look different</u> to followers of other religions, and be more <u>unified</u>.

The *Five Ks* are...

① Kesh (uncut hair)

<u>Kesh</u> is the practice of allowing <u>hair</u> to <u>grow naturally</u> instead of cutting it. This is a symbol of <u>respect</u> for the <u>perfection</u> of God's creation. The uncut long hair is often covered with a <u>turban</u>.

② Kangha (a wooden comb)

The small comb is used <u>twice a day</u> to ensure that the <u>hair</u> is kept <u>tidy</u>. It reminds Sikhs of the importance of <u>cleanliness</u> and <u>self-discipline</u>.

③ Kara (a steel bracelet)

The kara is a symbol of <u>strength</u>, <u>honesty</u> and God's <u>eternal nature</u>. It reminds Sikhs that all of their actions should be <u>in line</u> with the <u>teaching</u> of the <u>gurus</u>.

④ Kachera (cotton underwear)

The kachera symbolises the importance of <u>chastity</u> and <u>self-control</u>. Both <u>men and women</u> are expected to wear the simple <u>cotton shorts</u>.

⑤ Kirpan (a ceremonial sword)

The kirpan was originally a <u>sword</u> for <u>self-defence</u>. The <u>ceremonial kirpan</u> is worn today as a reminder that Sikhs should <u>fight</u> against <u>injustice</u> and <u>protect</u> the <u>weak</u>.

Each of the Five Ks symbolises something different

The Five Ks were intended by Guru Gobind Singh to make Sikhs different to followers of other religions, as well as to remind them of their commitment to live in the proper way.

The Significance of Religious Artefacts

Artefacts are special <u>physical items</u> used by <u>religious believers</u>.

Artefacts come in all Shapes and Sizes

1) <u>Artefacts</u> are items that have a <u>special importance</u> to followers of a <u>religion</u>.
2) Many different types of items can be classed as artefacts, including <u>clothes</u>, <u>books</u> and <u>food</u>.
3) Copies of <u>holy scriptures</u> — e.g. the <u>Bible</u> or the <u>Qur'an</u> — are artefacts.
4) <u>Statues</u> of religious figures — e.g. the <u>Buddha</u>, a <u>Hindu god</u> or the <u>Virgin Mary</u> — are also artefacts.

Some Artefacts are used in Worship and Festivals

1) <u>Special clothing</u> is worn by members of several religions, often as a sign of <u>respect</u> to God. Some Jews wear a <u>tallit</u> (prayer shawl) at the <u>synagogue</u> to remind them of their <u>duty</u> to G-d. Special <u>robes</u> are worn by some Christian vicars, priests and monks.
2) <u>Muslims</u> use <u>prayer mats</u> when they pray so that they can ensure they are praying on a <u>clean</u> piece of <u>ground</u>.

Priests wear special robes for worship.

3) <u>Food</u> can be a religious artefact, e.g. <u>karah parshad</u>. This is a <u>Sikh dish</u> made of flour, butter and sugar which is served to <u>visitors</u> at the gurdwara (see p.75). It is considered a <u>gift</u> from <u>Waheguru</u>.
4) Artefacts are also frequently used to help <u>celebrate</u> religious <u>festivals</u>. Hindus buy special <u>powders</u> to throw over each other at the <u>Holi</u> festival, Jews have specific <u>tablecloths</u> and <u>crockery</u> for the <u>Passover meal</u>, and Christians use <u>advent candles</u> to count down the days to <u>Christmas</u>.

Lots of Artefacts are found in the Home

1) Many religious believers have artefacts in their <u>homes</u> to <u>remind</u> them of <u>God</u>, or to help them <u>interact</u> with <u>God</u>.
2) <u>Prayer beads</u> are used by lots of believers to help them <u>pray</u>.
3) Some <u>Buddhists</u> hang <u>prayer flags</u> to bring <u>blessings</u> to the house.
4) <u>Orthodox</u> Christians often have <u>icons</u> (paintings of Jesus, Mary, saints or angels) in their homes to remind them of <u>God's presence</u> and to help them <u>pray</u>.
5) Most Hindus have a <u>murti</u> (an image of a god) in their homes to help them <u>worship</u>.

Artefacts are important to religious believers

Artefacts have various purposes and uses. Some are used in prayer, worship or festivals, and others simply remind believers of their faith. All artefacts have to be treated with respect.

Questions

Here are a few questions to check that you've been paying attention over the past few pages...

Warm-up Questions

1) State one of the key questions that religious thinkers ask about God.
2) What is the key difference between Jewish and Christian beliefs about Jesus?
3) 'Waheguru' is a name used to describe God in which religion?
4) Which religion is the Star of David a symbol of?

Practice Questions

The five questions coming up might take you a bit longer to deal with.

1) Copy out and complete this passage, adding the correct words from the list below:

omniscient   **Trinity**   **omnipotent**   **creator**   **one**   **omnipresent**

Jews believe that there is only _____ G-d who was the _____
of the Universe and everything in it. They believe that G-d is holy, merciful and
_____ (all-powerful), as well as being _____ (all knowing).
Unlike Christians, Jews don't believe in the _____. They also believe that
they shouldn't draw pictures of G-d. Both Christians and Jews believe that God/G-d is
_____ (everywhere) and that he has given humans free will.

2) Are these statements true or false?
   a) Muslims believe that Shaytan tries to lead them away from Allah.
   b) The Mool Mantar is an important teaching for Jews.
   c) Buddhists believe in a creator god.
   d) There are three main parts of the khanda symbol.

3) Explain why the number three is an important part of the Om symbol.

4) Briefly explain what each of the items below is, and what it symbolises.
   a) kangha   b) kara   c) kachera

5) Copy and complete this table, putting the symbols and artefacts into the correct column.

Christianity	Islam	Judaism	Hinduism	Sikhism	Buddhism

dharmachakra   **Om**   **tallit**   **nishan sahib**
ichthus   **Torah**   **karah parshad**   **advent candles**
murti   **star and crescent**   **cross**   **khanda**

Sacred Texts: The Bible

Sacred texts provide believers with <u>encouragement from God</u>, <u>guidance</u> for life and even <u>laws</u> for whole countries.

*Sacred texts contain the **Word of God***

1) Most religions have one or more <u>sacred texts</u> that form the <u>basis</u> of the religion.
2) Sometimes a text is considered to be <u>The Word of God</u> — God's ultimate <u>message</u> to humankind. In this case, it has great <u>authority</u> and can't be <u>changed</u>, <u>altered</u> or <u>rejected</u>.
3) Many religious people believe that spending time <u>reading</u> their sacred text is the best way to <u>learn</u> about their God and to <u>draw closer</u> to him.
4) <u>Passages</u> of sacred texts are often <u>read aloud</u> as part of religious <u>worship</u>.
5) Religious believers often try to <u>learn</u> part or all of their sacred texts <u>by heart</u>, to help them worship God even when they don't have a copy of the text with them.

*The **Bible** is split into the **Old** and **New Testaments***

1) The <u>Bible</u> is the Christian sacred text. It's also referred to as the <u>Holy Scriptures</u>.
2) The Bible is a collection of several different works, called <u>books</u>, written in a variety of <u>different styles and languages</u> over a period of at least 1000 years.
3) Most Christians believe that the Bible was <u>inspired by God</u> and written down by a series of <u>human authors</u>.

4) The books of the Bible are divided into two main parts — the <u>Old Testament</u> and <u>New Testament</u>:

The Old Testament

The Old Testament is the <u>Jewish Scriptures</u> (Jews consider it to be sacred). It was written in Hebrew and Aramaic languages, and its books include the <u>Creation</u> story, the books of the <u>Law</u> (<u>Torah</u>), the <u>10 Commandments</u>, various <u>histories</u> of Ancient Israel, <u>prophecy</u>, <u>poetry</u> and <u>psalms</u>.

The New Testament

The New Testament is the specifically <u>Christian</u> part of the Bible. Its 27 books were written in <u>Greek</u> in the 1st century CE. They include the <u>4 Gospels</u>, the <u>Acts</u> of the Apostles (describing the early years of Christianity) and a series of letters from <u>St Paul</u> and other Christian leaders giving <u>advice</u> about the Christian life and Church. The final book of the New Testament is the book of <u>Revelation</u>, a <u>vision</u> about the end of the world.

The Bible is sacred to Christians

The Bible is made up of many books, written by lots of different people. Even the New Testament was written almost 2000 years ago, but it's still read by millions of Christians today.

Sacred Texts: The Bible

Christians look to the Bible for <u>help</u> and <u>guidance</u>. It tells them about the life of <u>Jesus</u>, who they believe is the best possible <u>example</u> for how to live a <u>moral life</u>.

The Bible is used as a *Christian Faith Guidebook*

1) Christians look to the Bible as a <u>guide</u> for <u>how</u> they should <u>live</u> their lives.

2) It presents <u>Jesus</u> as an <u>example</u> for living a <u>godly</u>, <u>moral life</u>, and teaches that Christians should aim to <u>love each other</u> just like God loves them.

3) Lots of the <u>rituals</u> that churches use in <u>worship</u> come from the Bible, e.g. the <u>Eucharist</u> (<u>Mass</u> or <u>Holy Communion</u>) and <u>baptism</u>.

4) The Roman Catholic Church does use the Bible, but Catholic <u>tradition</u> and the teachings of the <u>Pope</u> are also very important for guidance.

5) The Bible is read in <u>church</u> during <u>worship</u>. Christians also <u>study</u> it on their own and in groups for <u>guidance</u>.

Christians *Interpret* the Bible in *Different Ways*

Different groups of Christians <u>interpret</u> the Bible in <u>different</u> ways:

1 Fundamentalists

These Christians believe that <u>everything</u> written in the Bible is <u>literally true</u>, e.g. that God created the world in six days.

> Some people argue that there are contradictions in the Bible, and so it's impossible for everything in it to be literally true.

2 Conservatives

They believe that the Bible was <u>inspired</u> by God, but that the writers' own interests also come through. Readers must use their <u>intelligence</u> (a gift from God) and the guidance of the <u>Holy Spirit</u> in order to understand the text.

3 Liberals

They believe that many things in the Bible should be interpreted <u>symbolically rather than literally</u>. For example, when Jesus healed a blind man, they think the story means Jesus helped him to 'see' the truth.

Christians use the Bible in worship and in everyday life

Although they may sometimes disagree about exactly how to interpret the Bible, all Christians believe that it should have authority in their lives and influence over their actions.

Sacred Texts: The Torah

The term 'Torah' can be a bit confusing — some Jews refer to the Old Testament as the Torah, others mean just the first five books of it. Then there's also the Oral Torah...

Jews have a **Written Torah** and an **Oral Torah**

1) Jewish scriptures consist of the 'Written Torah' (Tenakh) and the 'Oral Torah'.
2) The Tenakh is the 'Jewish Bible' — it's basically the same as the Christian Old Testament, but some of the books are in a different order.
3) The 'Oral Torah' is an enormous body of Jewish teachings that has been collected and written down over the centuries.

The **Tenakh** contains a **Mixture** of writings

1) The first five books of the Tenakh are referred to as the Torah, in the narrow sense, and contain the 613 mitzvot (commandments) that were given to Moses by G-d.
2) Jews consider this Torah to be the holiest part of the Tenakh.
3) The rest of the Tenakh includes the history of the Israelites after the death of Moses, as told by the prophets. There are also the psalms (prayers and hymns) and proverbs (wise sayings).

The **Oral Torah** has been built up over the **Centuries**

1) The Talmud forms the majority of the Oral Torah. It consists of the teachings and opinions of thousands of rabbis (Jewish teachers), as well as a commentary on those writings.
2) Orthodox Jews, however, believe that some of the Talmud was given to Moses directly by G-d.
3) Today, panels of rabbis give responses to tricky questions that aren't covered in existing writings, e.g. whether Jews should drive on the Sabbath. This is a kind of Oral Torah.

The Torah is **Read** aloud at the **Synagogue**

1) The Torah scrolls are kept in the Aron Kodesh (the Ark — see p.70) in the synagogue, and sections are read from it three times a week — on Mondays, Thursdays and Saturdays.
2) Over the course of the year, the entire Torah (the first five books of the Tenakh) is read.
3) The sections are usually read by a rabbi or a trained reader, so it is a great honour for a regular member of the congregation to be asked to read.

The term 'Torah' means different things to different people

Some Jews use the word 'Torah' to refer to the whole Tenakh; to others it's just the first section of the Tenakh. The term can also be used to refer to the whole, vast body of Jewish teachings.

Sacred Texts: The Torah

Just as Christians have different interpretations of the Bible, there are a <u>variety</u> of ways in which Jews <u>interpret</u> the Torah, and <u>opinions vary</u> on how strictly it should be followed.

Orthodox Jews *live Strictly by the Torah*

1) The word '<u>Orthodox</u>' means 'right belief'. Orthodox Jews believe that <u>traditional</u> Jewish beliefs and practices are still important <u>today</u>.

2) Orthodox Jews believe that the <u>Torah</u> and parts of the <u>Talmud</u> were given to Moses <u>directly</u> by G-d, so they should be strictly followed.

3) Around <u>65%</u> of British Jews who are synagogue members belong to an Orthodox synagogue, though they don't all follow the Torah <u>to the same extent</u>.

Progressive Jews *interpret the Torah Less Rigidly*

1) In <u>Britain</u> there are two 'progressive' Jewish movements — <u>Reform</u> and <u>Liberal Judaism</u>.

2) <u>Progressive Jews</u> apply the Torah to <u>modern life</u> in a different way to Orthodox Jews. They believe that the written Torah is people's <u>interpretations</u> of the word of G-d, not that word itself.

3) They believe that the <u>moral commandments</u> must be followed (although they are open to <u>interpretation</u>), but the <u>ritual laws</u> can be <u>adapted</u> or <u>abandoned</u> in response to changes in society.

4) When the Torah was written down, the Jewish people consisted of a number of <u>tribes</u> living in the <u>wilderness</u>. Progressive Jews believe that what was true for them is not necessarily true for urban Jews living in the <u>21st century</u>.

Jewish laws are called *Mitzvot*

1) Judaism teaches that Jews should obey the <u>laws</u> of the land they <u>live in</u>, as well as the <u>613 mitzvot</u> (commandments) in the Torah.

2) <u>Justice</u> is an important part of Judaism and features heavily in the Torah — in terms of what's due to <u>G-d</u>, and to fellow <u>Jews</u>.

3) Special courts (<u>Bet Din</u>) exist in many countries to settle <u>Jewish disputes</u>.

4) The Torah is filled with details of <u>laws</u>, <u>rewards</u> and <u>punishments</u>. But for many modern Jews, the punishments listed in the Torah are considered <u>too extreme</u>.

The Torah is interpreted differently by different Jewish groups

Much of the Torah was written down thousands of years ago, so it's not surprising that some Jews find some of its teachings and rituals difficult to follow in the 21st century.

Sacred Texts: The Qur'an

Muslims believe that the Qur'an is the most <u>important</u> book in the world, as it records the <u>exact words of Allah</u>, which were revealed to the <u>Prophet Muhammad</u>.

Muslims believe that the **Qur'an**...

(1) ...is a **complete** record of **Allah's words**

The Prophet Muhammad never <u>forgot</u> any of Allah's revelations, and his followers recorded them <u>at once</u> and learned them <u>by heart</u>.

(2) ...is a totally **accurate** and **unchanged** record

Caliph Uthman (an early Muslim ruler) made sure there was only <u>one</u> version of the Qur'an and that it was completely <u>correct</u>.

(3) ...is a complete guide to **Islamic life**

The Qur'an says what Muslims must <u>believe</u>, and how they must <u>live</u>, in order to get to <u>Paradise</u>. In the Qur'an, Allah tells Muslims what they need to know, so that they can please him. Since Muslims believe the Qur'an came directly from Allah, they trust it <u>completely</u>.

(4) ...must always be **read** in **Arabic**

Allah gave the Qur'an to the Prophet Muhammad in <u>Arabic</u>. If you read it in another language, you might not get the <u>proper</u> meaning. So Muslims must <u>learn</u> Arabic to be sure they are reading the <u>real</u> Qur'an.

The **Qur'an** is treated with **Great Respect**

Because the Qur'an is so important, Muslims treat it with great <u>respect</u>. Most Muslim households own a copy of the Qur'an and will:

1) keep their Qur'an <u>wrapped up</u> to keep it clean.
2) <u>wash their hands</u> before touching it.
3) keep it on a <u>higher shelf</u> than all other books.
4) place it on a <u>special stand</u> when they read it.

> **The Qur'an is read during private prayers at home and public prayers at the mosque, so Muslims get to know it really well. In the month of <u>Ramadan</u> (see p.62), the Qur'an is read from <u>beginning to end</u> during worship at the mosque.**

Muslims believe that the Qur'an is the word of Allah

When Muslims read the Qur'an, they're learning about what Allah's like, how he relates to humans, and how to live the way he wants so that they can get to Paradise.

Sacred Texts: The Qur'an

The Qur'an is supplemented by the Hadith. Muslims don't believe that these writings are the direct word of Allah, but that they are sayings and practices of the Prophet Muhammad.

The Qur'an is divided into **114 Surahs**

1) The Qur'an is organised into 114 surahs (chapters).
2) The surahs are arranged in order of length — from the longest to the shortest, apart from surah 1, the Fatihah, which is a short statement of important Islamic beliefs.
3) Each surah is made up of Ayat (verses).
4) Most surahs begin with the Bismillah. This is an Arabic phrase meaning 'In the name of Allah, the Entirely Merciful, the Especially Merciful.' This means that when Muslims start to read any surah, they are reminded of the mercy of Allah.

Muslims also read the **Hadith**

1) After the Prophet Muhammad died, Muslim scholars gathered together a number of his sayings and teachings, which formed the Hadith.
2) The Hadith also includes things said or done in Muhammad's presence that he approved of or criticised, so that Muslims know whether these things are good or not.
3) The Sunnah, found in the Hadith, refers to Muhammad's rituals, habits and customs that Muslims should follow. These include praying five times a day and washing before prayer.

Sharia Law is based on the **Qur'an**, **Hadith** and **Sunnah**

1) Sharia law is a code of law which comes from the teachings of the Qur'an and the example of Muhammad found in the Hadith.
2) Some countries base their entire legal system on Sharia law, and Muslim communities in many countries use Sharia courts to settle family or business disputes.
3) Sharia law is not just about crime — there are rules and guidelines on all parts of life, including how Muslims should live in order to please Allah.

The Hadith and Sunnah are important to Muslims

The Qur'an is the most important and sacred part of Islam, but the Hadith and Sunnah are also important to Muslims as they show how the Prophet Muhammad lived.

Sacred Texts: The Guru Granth Sahib

The sacred text for Sikhs is the <u>Guru Granth Sahib</u>. It is considered so <u>important</u> that it has more <u>authority</u> over the Sikh religion than any living person.

The Guru Granth Sahib was **Compiled** by **Guru Arjan**

1) The Guru Granth Sahib is a collection of religious <u>hymns</u> and <u>poetry</u> and is considered to be the <u>head</u> of the Sikh religion.

2) Sikhs believe that the <u>message</u> contained within it is the word of <u>Waheguru</u> (see p.34), and that this message will help their souls develop.

3) The first edition of the text was compiled by <u>Guru Arjan</u>, the fifth guru, and it was completed by Guru Gobind Singh, the tenth guru (see p.23).

4) The hymns were written mostly by the <u>first five gurus</u>, but writings by <u>Hindus</u>, <u>Muslims</u> and <u>other Sikhs</u> are also included.

The **Sacred Text** took the **Place** of the **Living Gurus**

1) The tenth guru, <u>Guru Gobind Singh</u>, decided that the Guru Granth Sahib would <u>replace</u> the living gurus in <u>teaching</u> and <u>guiding</u> the Sikh religion.

2) Guru Gobind Singh <u>added</u> a number of <u>hymns</u> to the text, and then declared that <u>nothing</u> else could be added to it, as it contained all the <u>wisdom</u> that Sikhs would need.

Before the text became a guru, it was known as the <u>Adi Granth</u>.

3) The Guru Granth Sahib is <u>read regularly</u> by Sikhs, and is at the <u>centre</u> of all Sikh <u>ceremonies</u>, including baptisms, marriages and funerals.

It is **Treated** like a **Living Guru**

1) The Guru Granth Sahib is treated with a lot of <u>respect</u> — it is kept on a special covered <u>platform</u> in the <u>gurdwara</u> and is never placed on the ground. At night, it is put in a separate bed or cot.

2) Worshippers in the gurdwara must <u>bow</u> to the text and <u>never turn their backs</u> to it. However, Sikhs <u>don't worship</u> the Guru Granth Sahib — they are showing <u>respect</u> to it because it contains God's words.

3) When someone <u>reads</u> from the Guru Granth Sahib, they wave a <u>chauri</u> (a kind of fan) over it from time to time as another sign of <u>respect</u>.

4) The Guru Granth Sahib contains <u>moral</u> and <u>ethical</u> <u>guidance</u> and helps Sikhs find <u>unity with Waheguru</u>.

It is very <u>difficult</u> to treat the Guru Granth Sahib with the <u>proper respect</u>, and therefore many Sikhs <u>don't</u> own a copy of it. Instead, they might have a book of <u>poetry</u> written by Guru Gobind Singh, or a <u>prayer book</u>.

The Guru Granth Sahib must be shown great respect by Sikhs

Since Guru Gobind Singh decided that the Guru Granth Sahib would replace human gurus, it is treated as if it were a living guru itself. This is one reason why it's shown so much respect.

Sacred Texts in Hinduism and Buddhism

Buddhists and Hindus have a number of texts that are considered sacred.

Hinduism has Many sacred texts

1) Hindus have several different collections of sacred texts which are used in rituals and festivals, as well as for personal devotion.

2) The oldest and most sacred texts are known as the Vedas.

3) The Ramayana is an epic poem about Rama and Sita — two Hindu gods.

4) The Mahabharata is the longest epic poem in the world (see p.24) and contains the Bhagavad Gita — a popular song about the god Krishna and nobleman Arjuna.

5) All Hindu sacred texts are divided into two categories — shruti and smriti:

Shruti

These are texts that are believed to have been revealed to the holy men by God. Hindus believe that the shruti works, including the Vedas, have more authority than smriti books.

Smriti

These books are based on human memories and recollections of God's message. The Ramayana and Mahabharata are both smriti works. 'Smriti' is often translated as 'tradition' and the books often refer to the traditional rules of dharma (see p.59). Hindus are often more familiar with smriti books than shruti ones.

The Tipitaka is a collection of texts Sacred to many Buddhists

1) The Tipitaka (also known as the Pali Canon) is the earliest collection of writings based on the teachings of Buddha.

2) The name means 'three baskets'. This refers to the three baskets originally used to carry the texts which were written on loose leaves.

3) It's believed that the Buddha's disciples memorised many of his sermons and teachings and passed them on. They were only written down centuries later.

4) Many monks and priests recite from the Tipitaka during rituals, and many Buddhists use sections of the texts for meditation.

5) The Tipitaka consists of three 'baskets' (sections):

- The Sutta Pitaka is made up of some of Buddha's stories, anecdotes and advice for following the path to enlightenment.
- The Vinaya Pitaka contains guidelines and rules for monks and nuns.
- The Abhidhamma Pitaka is a philosophical text which explains Buddhist teachings.

Hindus and Buddhists have more than one sacred text

Hindus and Buddhists have many collections of texts that they consider to be sacred. They use these for personal development, morality and words for rituals and festivals.

The Importance of Prayer

Prayer comes in a variety of different forms, and varies from one religion to another.

Prayer puts people In Touch with their God

1) Prayer is when believers communicate with their god or gods. This can be done mentally or vocally.

2) Several religions have set prayers that people say together during an act of worship, e.g. the Lord's Prayer in Christianity and the Shema in Judaism.

3) But prayer can also be private — individuals communicate with God in silence, or in their own words.

4) Some prayers require specific movements, such as the Muslim salat (see p.53), where believers place their hands, knees and foreheads on the ground.

People pray for many Different Reasons

People from most religions pray regularly, for lots of different reasons:

1) Believers pray to give thanks for something, e.g. to thank God for providing their food.

2) They might pray for help, e.g. to ask God to bring peace to a region in crisis, or to help them with something in their daily lives.

3) People pray to ask God for forgiveness, e.g. if they have done something wrong.

Prayer can be a Powerful thing

1) Most religions teach that God listens to prayers, so it is common for believers to ask God for things when they pray, e.g. for someone to be healed.

2) Most religious people believe that God answers prayers, but there is then the problem of 'unanswered prayers', when God doesn't grant a believer's request.

3) Some people argue that God answers all prayers in his own way and in his own time. Others say that God knows best and does things for reasons that we don't understand.

Prayer is the way believers communicate with God

For many religious people, prayer is a really important part of their religion. In fact, some Christian monks and nuns believe prayer is so important that they dedicate their lives to it.

The Importance of Prayer: Christianity

Christian prayer is much <u>more</u> than just <u>asking</u> God for a load of stuff.

Private Prayer draws a Christian Closer to God

1) Christian prayer is <u>communication</u> with God — it can take place in <u>church</u> or in <u>private</u>.

2) Christians use prayer to deepen their <u>faith</u> in God. They do this by communicating with him and trying to <u>hear</u> what he's saying.

3) Different Christians use different <u>methods</u> to accomplish this:

The 'Quiet Time' — time spent <u>alone</u> with God, reading the Bible or praying.

Meditation — a form of prayer where the believer clears their mind of <u>distracting</u> thoughts and focuses on God. It sometimes involves <u>repeating</u> a prayer many times.

Contemplation — <u>wordless</u> prayer in which the believer senses God's <u>presence</u> strongly.

The Rosary — a string of beads <u>used</u> by Roman Catholic and Orthodox Christians. As the beads are moved through the fingers, prayers are said, e.g. the Lord's Prayer and the Ave Maria (Hail Mary).

Icons — <u>sacred pictures of saints</u> used by Orthodox Christians to help them focus on God. They are often kissed, but believers do not pray to the icons.

The Lord's Prayer is an important prayer for Christians

1) The <u>Lord's Prayer</u> is known and used by Christians around the world.

2) It is based on <u>Jesus's words</u> in Matthew's and Luke's Gospels, where he <u>instructs</u> his disciples <u>how</u> they should <u>pray</u>.

3) The prayer covers a number of key <u>themes</u> in Christianity, including the idea that God is our <u>Father</u>, that he <u>provides</u> for our physical needs, and that we must ask for his <u>forgiveness</u> for the things that we have done wrong.

4) Different <u>denominations</u> use slightly different <u>versions</u> of the Lord's prayer. Many add the ending: "For the kingdom, the power and the glory are yours, now and for ever. Amen."

"This, then, is how you should pray:
"'Our Father in heaven,
hallowed be your name,
your kingdom come,
your will be done,
on earth as it is in heaven.
Give us today our daily bread.
And forgive us our debts,
as we also have forgiven our debtors.
And lead us not into temptation,
but deliver us from the evil one.'
Matthew 6:9-13 NIV

Christians pray to develop their relationship with God

The Bible has several instances of Jesus praying and he talks about it quite a lot. Jesus gave the Lord's Prayer to his followers to help them pray, so it's pretty important to Christians.

The Importance of Prayer: Judaism

Jews also believe that they can <u>connect</u> with G-d through prayer.

Jews have **Three Special Times** for **Daily Prayer**

1) Jews have daily prayers at <u>three special times</u> — in the morning, afternoon and evening.
2) At these times, <u>men</u> will try to attend the <u>synagogue</u> and become part of a <u>minyan</u> — a group of at least ten, which is the minimum needed for a service.
3) <u>Women</u> normally pray at <u>home</u>, because they would traditionally have had domestic duties and were not permitted to form part of a minyan.
4) In Reform Judaism (see p.45), women <u>are allowed</u> to attend the synagogue for daily prayers and form part of a <u>minyan</u>.

The **Siddur** is the Jewish **Prayer Book**

1) The <u>Siddur</u> sets out the time of day for different prayers and contains some <u>set prayers</u>.
2) As well as the normal daily prayers, there are also <u>special prayers</u> for before and after eating and for getting up and going to bed. In fact, pretty much every <u>event</u> in life, good or bad, can be a <u>reason to pray</u>.
3) The Siddur also includes prayers for the <u>Shabbat</u> (Sabbath, or holy day of the week) and <u>festivals</u>, including marriages, naming ceremonies and funerals.

Jewish **Men** often wear a **Kippah** when praying

1) A <u>kippah</u> is a <u>skullcap</u> which is worn by Jewish <u>men</u> when they <u>pray</u>.
2) Many <u>Orthodox Jews</u> wear a kippah <u>throughout the day</u> to remind them that G-d's <u>intelligence</u> is vastly <u>higher</u> than ours.
3) Some Jews also wear <u>tefillin</u> while praying. These are <u>leather boxes</u> that contain passages from <u>scripture</u> and are <u>tied</u> to the head or arm during the morning prayer on weekdays.
4) The <u>tefillin</u> are worn to fulfil one of the <u>commandments</u> found in <u>Deuteronomy</u>:

> "Tie them [the commandments] as symbols on your hands and bind them on your foreheads." Deuteronomy 6:8 NIV

Jews have lots of set prayers

The Siddur has prayers for many different occasions, and Jews believe it's important to pray at regular points during the day. Prayer also plays an important part in Jewish communal worship.

The Importance of Prayer: Islam

Muslims pray <u>five times a day</u>, which helps them to keep their lives <u>focused</u> on Allah.

Prayer is a Pillar of Islam

1) Prayer is one of the most <u>important</u> things in Islam — to be a Muslim you must pray in the way that Muhammad did. Regular prayer reminds Muslims of their <u>duty</u> to <u>obey Allah</u>.

2) Muslims should pray at <u>five different times</u> during the day: at sunrise, in the early afternoon, in the late afternoon, after sunset and late at night.

3) The <u>muezzin</u> (p.72) calls Muslims to prayer from the <u>minaret</u> (tower) of a <u>mosque</u>. The call to prayer begins "Allahu Akbar..." ("God is Greatest...").

4) Ideally, prayer should take place in a <u>mosque</u>. If this isn't possible, then a <u>prayer mat</u> should be used to make a prayer place.

5) <u>Wudu</u> is an important <u>ritual</u> which must be completed before praying. It consists of <u>washing</u> exposed parts of the body <u>three times</u>, so that a Muslim is <u>pure</u> and <u>clean</u> when approaching Allah.

<u>Compulsory</u> prayer is known as 'salat'. Extra prayers are called 'du'a' and can be done at <u>any time</u>. In du'a prayers, <u>beads</u> can be used — 99 beads for the 99 names of Allah.

A Rak'ah is a Unit of prayer

1) There is a set <u>ritual</u> for prayer — each unit of prayer is known as a <u>rak'ah</u>.

2) Each rak'ah involves <u>standing</u>, then <u>kneeling</u>, then putting the <u>forehead</u> to the ground as a sign of <u>submission</u>.

3) There is a <u>set number</u> of rak'ah that a Muslim must complete during each session of prayer.

4) A Muslim should face <u>Makkah</u> (Muhammad's place of birth — the most holy place in Islam) when praying. The direction of Makkah is called the <u>qiblah</u> — Makkah is southeast from Britain.

There are several Benefits of Prayer

1) Prayer keeps Muslims in <u>close contact</u> with Allah, and stops them from <u>forgetting</u> him.

2) It's also an expression of <u>solidarity</u> — doing exactly the <u>same</u> as all other Muslims.

3) Prayer can also help to develop a Muslim's <u>moral</u> and <u>spiritual discipline</u>.

Muslims pray to Allah five times a day

Prayer is a massively important part of the Muslim faith. It must be done regularly and Muslims must complete specific rituals both before and during their prayers.

The Importance of Prayer: Sikhism

Sikhs <u>pray</u> and <u>meditate</u> to bring themselves <u>closer</u> to God and to <u>purify</u> their minds.

Prayer and Meditation are Different

1) The <u>Rehat Maryada</u> is a code of conduct for Sikhs. It says that Sikhs must take part in <u>daily prayer and meditation</u>.
2) <u>Prayer</u> is a <u>conversation</u> between human beings and God. Sikhs spend time <u>praising</u> God and asking that he will <u>bless</u> them as they go about their day.
3) <u>Meditation</u> involves a period of <u>deep thought</u> about God. It can be done <u>silently</u> or by <u>reciting words or passages</u> from the Guru Granth Sahib.
4) Both prayer and meditation require worshippers to <u>clear their minds</u> of all other things and <u>focus</u> entirely on God.

Sikhs should meditate First Thing in the Morning

1) Sikhs are expected to get up <u>early every morning</u> and <u>meditate</u> on the names or qualities of God. This is known as <u>Nam Simran</u>.
2) This meditation can include <u>deep contemplation</u>, <u>singing of hymns</u> and <u>chanting</u> the word '<u>Waheguru</u>'.
3) This allows Sikhs to achieve a sense of <u>peace</u> and a <u>connection</u> with God.
4) Guru Nanak taught that meditating on God's name and character was the best way for Sikhs to fight the <u>Five Thieves</u> — the five major weaknesses that humans display (desire, anger, greed, attachment to things, and pride).

Sikhs Pray at Different Times during the day

1) Sikhs have a number of <u>set prayers</u>. The prayers are usually made up of small passages (<u>banis</u>) from the Guru Granth Sahib or other writings of the gurus.
2) The <u>Japji Sahib</u> is considered to be the <u>most important</u> of the banis. It is a hymn written by <u>Guru Nanak</u>, and is recited <u>every morning</u> after meditation.
3) <u>Five banis</u> are recited in the morning, <u>one</u> in the evening and <u>one</u> at night-time.
4) Sikhs consider <u>Waheguru</u> to be a <u>friend</u> who cares for them, and so they spend time praying in order to spend time in Waheguru's company.
5) They also believe that the right prayer can give them <u>hope</u>, <u>confidence</u> and <u>courage</u>.

> ### *Sikhs are expected to pray and meditate every day*
> Prayer and meditation are slightly different things that help Sikhs to focus on God. They help the believer to combat the Five Thieves — desire, anger, greed, attachment to things, and pride.

Religious Beliefs & Daily Life: Christianity

Christians believe that their <u>faith</u> should <u>affect</u> the way that they live their lives.

Jesus set an *Example* for *Christians*

1) Christians believe that they should try to live in a similar way to <u>Jesus</u> — they look to him and to the rest of the <u>Bible</u> for <u>moral guidance</u>.

2) The Old Testament contains lots of <u>laws</u>, but Jesus <u>challenged</u> some of these, saying that the Jewish authorities had <u>missed the point</u> of them.

3) Jesus argued that the '<u>spirit</u>' of the law is more important than the '<u>letter</u>', meaning the goal it is seeking matters more than its precise details. He criticised the <u>Pharisees</u> (a group of influential Jews) for making following the <u>law</u> more important than <u>loving people</u> or doing the <u>right</u> thing.

4) Jesus taught that a person's <u>motivations</u> are also important — he told his followers that being <u>angry</u> with someone could be almost as bad as <u>killing</u> them.

5) Above all, Jesus wanted Christians to love. He <u>summed up</u> the aim of all of the <u>Old Testament laws</u> like this:

> **"Love the Lord your God with all your heart and with all your soul and with all your mind and with all your strength... Love your neighbour as yourself." Mark 12:30-31 NIV**

6) Jesus showed his <u>love</u> for humanity by dying on the cross to save humankind (see p.137). Christians believe that they must be willing to follow his example of <u>self-sacrifice</u> and <u>love</u>.

There are many ways Christians can *Serve God*

Christians believe that it is important to <u>serve God</u>, just as Jesus did. There are lots of ways that they can do this:

1) By <u>loving</u> and <u>respecting other people</u>, <u>helping</u> those in <u>need</u>, and speaking out against <u>injustice</u>.

2) Some Christians believe they have been given a <u>calling</u> from God to serve him in a particular way — this is known as a <u>vocation</u>.

3) For some, a vocation means becoming a <u>minister</u> or a <u>priest</u>. For others it may mean becoming a <u>monk</u> or a <u>nun</u>, and living a very simple life with a focus on <u>prayer</u>.

4) Many Christians believe that their vocation is a <u>normal job</u> where they can <u>help people</u> and have a <u>positive impact</u>, e.g. being a doctor, parent, teacher or social worker.

5) Lots of Christians <u>volunteer</u> with <u>charities</u> or <u>community organisations</u>. They see this as a way of showing <u>God's love</u> in a <u>practical</u> way, and serving God by loving his creation.

Jesus taught that love is more important than laws

Showing God's love to other people is an important way in which Christians can follow Jesus's example and serve God. This can be done in a variety of ways, and often through a vocation.

Religious Beliefs & Daily Life: Judaism

Jews look to the <u>Torah</u> and the <u>Talmud</u> for <u>guidance</u> on how they should live.

Morality matters in Judaism

1) The most famous <u>mitzvot</u> (commandments) are the <u>Ten Commandments</u>, but they're not the only ones. In total, there are <u>613</u> mitzvot which Jews must try to obey.

2) The mitzvot cover a variety of topics, e.g. the treatment of the <u>poor</u>, <u>family relationships</u>, what <u>foods</u> may be eaten, and how <u>business</u> should be conducted.

3) The mitzvot can be <u>divided</u> up in different ways:

- <u>248</u> of the mitzvot are <u>positive</u>, telling Jews what they should do.

- <u>365</u> mitzvot are <u>negative</u>, telling them what they shouldn't do.

- <u>Ritual</u> mitzvot list special things Jews must or must not do to avoid offending G-d.

- <u>Moral</u> (ethical) mitzvot are about a Jew's dealings with <u>other people</u>.

4) <u>Observant</u> Jews think it's vital to live by a <u>moral code</u>. They will generally consider someone to be moral if they combine <u>religious observance</u> with <u>concern for other people</u>.

5) In deciding how to behave, Jews look first to the <u>Torah</u> for moral guidance, then to the <u>Talmud</u> (see p.44) and then to the wider body of traditional <u>Jewish teaching</u>.

6) Individual Jews may also seek the <u>advice</u> of another Jew who is more <u>knowledgeable</u> or wise in a particular area, especially a <u>rabbi</u> (teacher).

G-d will Forgive Jews if they are Sorry

1) Jews realise that no one can live by all 613 mitzvot all of the time. But they believe that G-d is <u>merciful</u> and will always forgive someone who is truly <u>sorry</u> for their <u>sins</u>.

2) The festival of <u>Yom Kippur</u> (see p.61) reminds Jews to ask for G-d's <u>forgiveness</u>.

3) For <u>Reform Jews</u>, an individual's <u>conscience</u> is the most important source of moral authority. They should use the traditional sources of authority, but then <u>decide for themselves</u>.

4) <u>Orthodox Jews</u> mostly believe that <u>correct</u> moral judgements are to be found by sticking as closely as possible to <u>traditional Jewish teaching</u>.

There are 613 mitzvot that Jews must try to obey

Different groups of Jews have different opinions on how much the 613 mitzvot must still be followed, but all Jews seek forgiveness from G-d when they have sinned.

Religious Beliefs & Daily Life: Islam

Muslims look to the Qur'an and the writings about the life of the Prophet Muhammad to see how they should behave and live their lives.

Muslims follow the **Qur'an** and **Muhammad's Example**

1) Allah didn't want human beings to ruin their lives, so he gave messages to angels, who passed his words on to prophets. These prophets delivered the words of Allah to the people on Earth.

2) Allah sent many prophets as messengers, but Muhammad was the last prophet, and Allah revealed the Qur'an to him.

3) As Allah's last prophet, Muslims regard Muhammad as the perfect example of a moral, trustworthy person, who they should try to be like.

4) Collections of Muhammad's sayings (the Hadith — see p.47) are a source of moral and spiritual guidance for many Muslims.

5) The Hadith contains the Sunnah (see p.47) — Muhammad's rituals, habits and customs, which are a model for a good Muslim life.

Khalifah — Taking Responsibility in Allah's name

1) Muslims believe that they have a duty to obey Allah.

2) Allah has laid down rules for living a moral life in the Qur'an (e.g. rules on dress, money and food), so any Muslim who doesn't obey these rules is disobeying Allah.

3) Muslims believe that they will pay for any disobedience on Judgement Day, when Allah will judge us on the basis of our actions.

4) Muslims also believe that we have been appointed Khalifah (trustees) of the Earth.

5) This means that while on Earth, we should take responsibility for the world in Allah's name, and make it the sort of place he wants it to be. This sometimes means applying the teachings of the Qur'an to new situations, and relying on our conscience to tell us what's right and wrong.

Muslims must live a moral life to please Allah

Muslims believe that Allah has given them directions for living a life that pleases him. They must follow those directions and look after the Earth to ensure that they are obeying Allah.

Religious Beliefs & Daily Life: Sikhism

Sikhs believe that spending <u>time</u> and <u>money</u> to <u>serve the community</u> is important.

Sewa means Selfless Service

1) The <u>Guru Granth Sahib</u> teaches that Sikhs should <u>serve others</u>. This concept is called <u>sewa</u>.
2) Sewa must be done <u>selflessly</u>, and <u>not</u> with any kind of <u>reward</u> in mind.
3) Sikhs believe that they are serving <u>God</u> by serving <u>other people</u> in the community, and so sewa is a form of <u>worship</u>.

There are Three Types of sewa

(1) Tan — **physical** service

This usually takes place at the <u>gurdwara</u>, and can include working in the <u>langar</u> (kitchen), <u>cleaning shoes</u> or <u>sweeping</u> the floor. Sikhs consider tan to be the most <u>important</u> part of sewa because Sikhs are told in the Guru Granth Sahib to <u>serve</u> using their <u>hands</u> and <u>feet</u>.

(2) Man — **mental** service

Sikhs believe that they should <u>contribute</u> to the Sikh community and to the wider society by using their <u>talents</u>, e.g. their <u>creativity</u> or their <u>organisational skills</u>.

(3) Dhan — **material** service

Sikhs are expected to make a <u>financial donation</u> to the <u>gurdwara</u> as a gift to the <u>gurus</u>, which is then distributed to the <u>poor</u> and to the <u>community</u>. This payment is known as the <u>dasvandh</u> and is expected to be <u>one tenth</u> of a Sikh's <u>earnings</u>.

Sewa Benefits the Community and the Individual

1) Sewa is intended to make a <u>positive impact</u> in the <u>community</u> and to help improve the <u>welfare</u> of all people.
2) Sikhs volunteer in <u>hospitals</u>, <u>nursing homes</u> and <u>community centres</u> to help organisations and individuals on a spiritual and physical level.
3) Although people who complete sewa should <u>not be aiming</u> to receive a <u>reward</u>, Sikhs believe that sewa can <u>develop</u> and <u>spiritually fulfil</u> them.
4) This is because they believe that you <u>become</u> more like the person you <u>serve</u>, and so if you are <u>serving God</u>, you become more <u>like God</u>.

Sikhs serve the community with their body, mind and money

Tan, man and dhan — three words for you to learn. The words may be simple, but they're an important part of Sikhism, as they enable Sikhs to serve God, each other and the community.

Religious Beliefs & Daily Life: Hinduism / Buddhism

Hindus and Buddhists seek to live <u>moral lives</u> that have a <u>positive effect</u> on the <u>world</u>.

Hindus believe they must live a Moral Life

1) Hindus believe that they must live in a way which <u>serves God</u> and <u>humanity</u>.

2) This principle is referred to as '<u>dharma</u>', which means '<u>duty</u>'.

3) There are several different types of dharma — one which is about <u>serving God</u>, one which relates to the <u>duties</u> of the <u>individual</u>, and one which is a general <u>moral code</u>.

4) People of different <u>ages</u>, <u>social positions</u> and <u>genders</u> have <u>different responsibilities</u> and are expected to <u>act differently</u>.

5) It is important for Hindus to <u>look after</u> other <u>people</u> and the <u>environment</u>. By doing this, they are also <u>serving God</u>.

Following Dharma generates Good Karma

1) The law of <u>karma</u> states that <u>every action</u> will have a <u>reaction</u> in the <u>future</u>. <u>Good actions</u> will have a <u>good effect</u>, and <u>bad actions</u> will have a <u>bad effect</u>.

2) Hindus believe that karma can <u>transfer</u> across <u>lifetimes</u>, so the <u>effects</u> may not be felt until the person has been <u>reincarnated</u>.

3) The <u>ten yamas</u> and <u>ten niyamas</u> are lists of <u>ethical rules</u> that some Hindus use to work out <u>how</u> they should live.

4) The <u>yamas</u> are a list of <u>guidelines</u> including what <u>not to do</u>, such as <u>lying</u>, <u>stealing</u> and being <u>violent</u>, and also what Hindus <u>should do</u>, such as being <u>patient</u> and <u>compassionate</u>.

5) The <u>niyamas</u> are a list of <u>positive</u> things that <u>should be done</u>, including <u>giving generously</u>, <u>worshipping God</u> and being <u>self-disciplined</u>.

Sila is part of a Moral Code for Buddhists

1) <u>Buddhists</u> believe that they should follow the <u>Noble Eightfold Path</u> to move towards <u>enlightenment</u> (see p.110).

2) <u>Sila</u> includes <u>three sections</u> of the path — right <u>speech</u>, right <u>action</u> and right <u>livelihood</u>.

3) Buddhists should <u>speak</u> in a way that is <u>honest</u>, <u>helpful</u> and <u>positive</u>.

4) They should <u>act ethically</u>, which includes <u>not hurting</u> any living thing.

5) The concept of <u>right livelihood</u> means doing a <u>job</u> that <u>doesn't</u> cause any <u>harm</u> to <u>humans</u>, <u>animals</u> or the <u>environment</u>.

6) Buddhists also follow the <u>precepts</u> (see p.20).

Serving God is an important part of being a Hindu

Dharma is an important concept in Hinduism — believers should act in a way which serves others and God. Buddhists have similar moral and ethical codes, but they do not involve God.

Religious Festivals: Christianity

Christians have two main festivals each year — <u>Christmas</u> and <u>Easter</u>.

Christmas is a celebration of Jesus's Birth...

1) Christmas is celebrated by most Christians on <u>25th December</u> and marks the <u>incarnation</u> — when <u>God's son</u> came to Earth as a human being.

2) Christmas comes after a period called <u>Advent</u>, which begins <u>four Sundays before Christmas</u>. This is a time of <u>preparation</u> for Christmas.

3) Lots of Roman Catholic, Orthodox and Anglican churches have a '<u>Midnight Mass</u>' to welcome Christmas Day, and most Christians go to church on <u>Christmas morning</u> to <u>celebrate</u>.

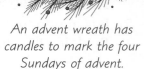

4) <u>Gifts</u> are exchanged to symbolise the fact that Jesus was <u>God's gift</u> to the world, and to reflect the gifts that the <u>Magi</u> (wise men) brought Jesus when he was born.

An advent wreath has candles to mark the four Sundays of advent.

5) Some Christians dislike modern Christmas <u>traditions</u> and <u>customs</u>, e.g. the character of <u>Santa Claus</u> (Father Christmas), giving <u>expensive presents</u> and <u>excessive eating</u> and <u>drinking</u>. They believe that some of these modern traditions <u>devalue</u> the <u>true meaning</u> of Christmas.

...and Easter is a celebration of his Resurrection

Easter is the most <u>important</u> festival for Christians, since it celebrates <u>Jesus's victory</u> over death, when God raised him <u>back to life</u> after his crucifixion. The lead-up to <u>Easter Sunday</u>, the day of resurrection, is marked by a number of important events:

Lent

Lent commemorates the <u>40 days and nights</u> Jesus spent <u>fasting</u> (going without food) in the <u>wilderness</u>. Rich foods are eaten up on <u>Shrove Tuesday</u> before Lent begins on <u>Ash Wednesday</u>. Some Christians give up <u>luxuries</u> during Lent, which is traditionally a time of self-denial.

Palm Sunday

On the Sunday before Easter, Christians remember Jesus's <u>triumphant entry</u> into Jerusalem. This marks the beginning of <u>Holy Week</u> — Jesus's final week <u>on Earth</u>.

Maundy Thursday & Good Friday

<u>Maundy Thursday</u> commemorates the <u>Last Supper</u> held on the night before Jesus died. <u>Good Friday</u> recalls Jesus's <u>crucifixion</u> — special services are held, particularly on Friday afternoon.

Easter Sunday

<u>Easter Sunday</u> is a <u>joyous</u> occasion when Jesus's resurrection is celebrated. Some churches hold services on the Saturday night, and most have <u>special services</u> on the Sunday morning.

Christmas and Easter are holy days for Christians

Both of these festivals have lots of cultural customs attached to them, e.g. stockings and Easter eggs. For Christians, they are two extremely important and special religious celebrations.

Religious Festivals: Judaism

Yom Kippur, Pesach (Passover) and Hanukkah are just some of the festivals celebrated by Jews.

Yom Kippur involves Fasting

1) Yom Kippur (the Day of Atonement) is one of the most important festivals in the Jewish calendar.

2) It takes place ten days after the start of the Jewish New Year, which falls in September or October. It involves fasting for 25 hours — from half an hour before nightfall on the day before Yom Kippur until half an hour after nightfall on the day itself.

3) During this time, Jews don't eat or drink anything, not even water. This is to help them focus entirely on spiritual, rather than physical, matters.

4) The festival gives Jews the opportunity to ask G-d to forgive the sins they've committed over the past year.

Hanukkah is the Festival of Light

1) Hanukkah is a festival which lasts for eight days and eight nights. It takes place on different days each year, but it falls sometime in November or December.

2) The festival commemorates the recapturing of Jerusalem by the Jews after it had been taken by the King of Syria.

3) When the Jews finished repairing the Temple in Jerusalem, they lit the menorah (lamp) as a symbol of G-d's presence. The menorah burnt for eight days, even though there was only enough oil for one day — this was considered a miracle.

4) During Hanukkah, Jews light one candle each day on a special nine-branched menorah, with the candle in the centre being used to light each of the other eight.

5) Special prayers are said, songs are sung and fried foods are eaten during the festival. Some Jews also exchange gifts such as chocolate money and special spinning tops.

Pesach (Passover) commemorates the Exodus

1) Pesach (Passover) takes place in March or April each year. It remembers the night before the Exodus — when Moses led the Israelites (Jews) from slavery in Egypt to freedom.

2) On that night, the angel of death killed the first-born sons of all the Egyptians, but 'passed over' the Israelites' houses without entering to harm them.

3) Jews celebrate the Passover with a Seder meal — this includes bread made without yeast, bitter herbs, and a lamb bone and a roasted egg (which aren't eaten). Each of the foods symbolises a different part of the story, which is retold by the head of the family during the meal.

Jews celebrate different festivals throughout the year

These three Jewish festivals commemorate very different things. Make sure you know the name of each festival, what it is for, and the way in which it's celebrated by Jewish believers.

Religious Festivals: Islam

Ramadan is the most important time of the Islamic year and involves fasting for a month. It ends with the festival of Eid ul-Fitr.

Ramadan is a Pillar of Islam

1) Muslims must fast between sunrise and sunset during the month of Ramadan in the Muslim calendar.

2) This fasting means no food, drink, smoking or sex. Ramadan is a time of physical and moral self-discipline, and a time of total obedience to Allah.

3) It's supposed to help Muslims understand hunger, which should make them more willing to help others.

4) Ramadan is also a time when Muslims can show publicly that Allah matters more than their physical needs.

5) Families and friends often spend lots of time together during Ramadan, particularly each evening when the fast is ended with a special meal called iftar.

There are exceptions to the rules:

1) Children don't have to fast until they're about 12 years old.

2) People can be excused for medical reasons, and medicine may be taken.

3) If you're on a journey, you can be excused. But you must make up the missed days later.

Eid ul-Fitr marks the End of Ramadan

1) Eid ul-Fitr is a festival of celebration which marks the end of the month of Ramadan.

2) Muslim families eat a rich meal together — the first daytime meal for a month.

3) There are special services at the Mosque, new clothes are bought, and money is given to charity.

4) Muslims also thank Allah for giving them help and self-control during Ramadan.

Eid ul-Adha is a Festival of Sacrifice

1) Eid ul-Adha commemorates Ibrahim's willingness to sacrifice his son to Allah.

2) Allah had appeared to Ibrahim in a dream and asked him to sacrifice his son, Isma'il, but then stopped Ibrahim just before he actually did it.

3) Allah provided Ibrahim with a lamb to sacrifice instead — Muslims remember this by sacrificing a sheep or a goat. The meat is shared out between family, friends and the poor.

4) The festival also marks the end of the annual Hajj pilgrimage to Makkah (see p.113).

Muslims fast during the daylight hours of Ramadan

Ramadan is a really important month for Muslims, as they spend time focusing on Allah rather than their physical needs. Remember that they do still eat and drink, but only when it's dark.

Religious Festivals: Sikhism

There are two types of Sikh festival: gurpurbs and melas.

Gurpurbs celebrate Important Events in the lives of the Gurus

1) Gurpurbs are festivals which celebrate the lives of the gurus (see p.23).
2) The festivals are celebrated joyfully, often with processions, music, martial arts and communal meals.
3) Gurdwaras are often decorated with flowers, flags and lights, and some give out sweets and other foods to the public.
4) Gurpurbs are also marked with an akhand path — a continuous reading of the Guru Granth Sahib, which takes 48 hours to complete.
5) Some of the most important gurpurbs include the birth of Guru Nanak, the birth of Guru Gobind Singh, the death of Guru Arjan and the death of Guru Tegh Bahadur.

Melas celebrate Events from Sikh History

Melas commemorate events from the history of the Sikh religion — they are opportunities for Sikhs to gather together to celebrate. Some of the most significant melas are:

Vaisakhi / Baisakhi

This is a harvest festival. It was given a new focus by Guru Gobind Singh, who founded the Khalsa (an inner group of dedicated Sikhs) during the festival. Many Sikhs join the Khalsa on this day by drinking, and being sprinkled with, Amrit, a special holy drink. The festival is the most important mela and marks the start of the Sikh new year. It is celebrated in a similar way to the gurpurbs, with music. There is also a lot of singing and chanting.

Diwali

Diwali (or Divali) is a festival of light which is also celebrated by Hindus (see p.64). For Sikhs, it is a time to remember when Guru Har Gobind and 52 Hindu princes were released from prison. On their return home, the Golden Temple was illuminated with many lights. Today, homes and shops are decorated with small lamps, and sweets are given out to everyone.

Hola Mohalla

This is an annual festival where Sikhs take part in martial arts displ
as music and poetry readings, over three days. The festival was st
Singh, who organised the first day of mock fighting in 1701. It w
for Sikhs to practise fighting, and it now reminds Sikhs to be bra

Gurpurbs and melas all mark important even

Sikh festivals are typically celebrated with lots of food, singi
most important rituals is an akhand path — an entire readi

Religious Festivals: Hinduism and Buddhism

Hindus and Buddhists have <u>many festivals</u> which are celebrated <u>throughout the year</u>.

Diwali is the Hindu festival of the New Year

1) Diwali is <u>Hindu festival of lights</u> that welcomes the <u>Hindu new year</u>.
   It lasts between 2 and 5 days.

2) It is usually held in <u>honour</u> of <u>Lakshmi</u> — the <u>goddess of wealth and prosperity</u>.
   Many Hindus <u>pray</u> to Lakshmi in the hope she will bring <u>good luck</u> for the year ahead.

3) The festival celebrates the <u>victory</u> of <u>light over darkness</u> and <u>goodness over evil</u>. People
   light <u>diyas</u> (small oil lamps) and place them outside to <u>celebrate</u> this spiritual victory.

4) <u>Fireworks</u> are let off during the evenings, and families and friends share <u>food and sweets</u>.
   Lots of <u>gifts</u> are bought and exchanged to celebrate the coming of a new year.

Hindus have many other festivals throughout the year. They often celebrate different <u>seasons</u>,
or remember different <u>gods</u>. Popular festivals include <u>Vasant Panchami</u> which celebrates the
<u>first day of spring</u> and <u>Krishna Janmashtami</u> which celebrates <u>Krishna's birthday</u>.

Buddhist festivals usually celebrate an Event in the Buddha's Life

Buddhists have <u>different festivals</u> depending on the <u>branch</u> of Buddhism they follow
and the <u>country</u> they live in. Some of the <u>most important</u> festivals include:

Parinirvana Day

This festival marks the <u>death</u> of the <u>Buddha</u>. Buddhists believe that the Buddha reached a
state of <u>enlightenment</u>, so his death meant he became <u>free</u> from the cycle of death and rebirth.
Buddhists celebrate the day by <u>chanting</u> and <u>meditating</u> in the <u>temple</u>. <u>Lights</u> in the temple are
<u>dimmed</u> and then made <u>bright</u>, showing that the light of the Buddha <u>shines on</u> in the world.

Wesak

Wesak celebrates the <u>Buddha's birth</u> and <u>enlightenment</u>, and in some forms of Buddhism,
his <u>death</u> as well. His enlightenment and death are said to have happened on his
birthday. Many Buddhists consider it to be their <u>most important festival</u>. Homes
are <u>decorated</u> and Buddhists visit the temple for <u>services</u>. <u>Water</u> is often <u>poured</u>
<u>over statues</u> of the Buddha to remind worshippers of the need to be <u>pure</u>.

Magha Puja

This festival remembers when <u>1250 disciples</u> came to see the Buddha without being
called. Buddhists use the day to try to <u>purify their minds</u> and do only <u>good deeds</u>.
It is often celebrated with <u>candlelit processions</u> around the temple's main hall.

lots of festivals that celebrate gods and seasons

cus on a god or the changing seasons. The Buddha is the most
m, so most Buddhist festivals celebrate a part of his life.

Questions

Religious texts, prayers and festivals... there's plenty for you to try and get your head around. Luckily, there are plenty of questions here to help you check how much you've learnt.

Warm-up Questions

1) Name the two sections that the Bible is divided into.
2) In which language should Muslims read the Qur'an?
3) Give two reasons why a religious believer might pray.
4) Name two of the melas (festivals) celebrated by Sikhs.
5) What does the Buddhist festival Wesak celebrate?

Practice Questions

Right then, time for some questions which might require a bit more brainpower.

1) Draw a table with three columns, labelled 'Christianity', 'Hinduism' and 'Islam'.
   Sort each of the terms below into the correct column.

   10 Commandments   **Hadith**   **Vedas**   **surahs**

   Sunnah   **Bhagavad Gita**   **Sharia law**   **Ramayana**

   New Testament   **Bismillah**   **gospels**

2) Briefly explain what each of the terms below refers to:
   a) Oral Torah   b) Adi Granth   c) Tipitaka

3) Copy out and complete this passage, adding the correct words from the list below:

   muezzin   wudu   Allah   Muhammad   Pillars   Makkah

   Prayer is one of the _____ of Islam and is very important to Muslims. They pray at least five times a day, and are called to prayer by the _____. Before they pray, each person must complete _____, which is the ritual of washing exposed parts of the body. Muslims believe that prayer keeps them in close contact with _____ and can develop their spiritual discipline. Whenever and wherever they pray, they must face in the direction of _____, the birthplace of _____.

4) Briefly explain the difference between prayer and meditation for Sikhs.

Questions

5) Copy and complete the passages below using the correct choice of words.

   a) **(Christians / Muslims)** try to follow Jesus's example in their daily lives. Jesus taught that loving people was **(less / more)** important than following the laws in the Old Testament. Jesus's **(birth / death)** was the ultimate example of self-sacrifice.

   b) Sewa is an important concept in **(Islam / Sikhism)** which involves serving others in a variety of ways. There are **(three / five)** types of sewa and they are intended to benefit both the community and the individual. **(Dhan / Tan)** is physical service and can include working in the **(langar / gurpurb)** (kitchen) of the gurdwara.

   c) **(Jews / Hindus)** believe in the law of karma, which states that all actions will have reactions in the future. This means that it's important to live a moral life and follow the principles of **(khalsa / dharma)** (religious duty). There is a list of **(five / ten)** yamas and ten **(niyamas / murtis)** which help believers to work out how they should live.

6) Describe briefly what is meant by the term 'vocation' in Christianity.

7) Put the days below in the order that they occur in the lead-up to Easter Sunday.

   Maundy Thursday   **Shrove Tuesday**   **Palm Sunday**   **Ash Wednesday**   **Good Friday**

8) Unscramble these religious festivals, and state which religion(s) each one belongs to.
   a) widlia
   b) kahuhnak
   c) restea
   d) daluediha

9) Read each of the sentences below and then match each one to an answer from Q8.
   i)   A sheep or goat is sacrificed to remember Ibrahim's willingness to sacrifice his son.
   ii) This festival marks the end of the season of Lent.
   iii) A festival of light celebrated by believers from more than one religion.
   iv) A festival of light which remembers the miraculous burning of an oil lamp in the Temple.

10) Choose one Buddhist festival and write a short description about what it celebrates and how it is celebrated by believers.

Section Three — Summary Questions

There's masses of stuff in this section and these summary questions are a great way to check how much of it you know. Have a go at all of the questions first, then if there are any you're not sure about, have a flick back through the section and swot up on the relevant pages.

1) Explain the difference between an 'immanent god' and a 'transcendent god'.

2) How many gods does a monotheistic religion believe in?

3) A politician says, "Religions make this country a better place."
    Explain how the politician could have no religious beliefs, but still believe this statement.

4) Explain why the Five Pillars of Islam are important to Muslims, naming at least one of the Pillars in your answer.

5) "God has many names and qualities, but only one form."
    Would this statement be made by a Sikh or a Hindu? Why?

6) What is the ichthus? Briefly describe how it became a religious symbol.

7) Explain why Hindus spend time chanting the word 'Om'.

8) Describe how the dharmachakra represents Buddhist beliefs and practices.

9) What are religious artefacts? Give an example of an artefact from each of three different religions in your answer.

10) Describe the difference between a fundamentalist interpretation and a liberal interpretation of the Bible.

11) Give three different types of writing that are included in the Tenakh.

12) Why was the Guru Granth Sahib given the title of Guru?

13) Choose one religious text and describe how it is treated specially.

14) "There's no point in praying — God can't hear you."
    Would a Christian agree with this statement? In your answer, briefly explain the importance of prayer to Christians.

15) Choose an item of special clothing worn by Jews and describe its use or importance in prayer or worship.

16) What is a rak'ah? Describe how a Muslim carries it out.

17) Why do Christians traditionally exchange gifts at Christmas? Give two reasons.

18) What is the purpose of the Muslim month of Ramadan?

19) Name the two different types of Sikh festival, and explain the difference between them.

20) "Religious festivals are all about presents and parties."
    Discuss this statement, including different points of view, as well as your own viewpoint.
    You should refer to a religion in your answer.

Churches — Christianity

Most religions have a special place where believers meet to <u>worship</u>.
For <u>Christians</u>, this place is usually a <u>church</u>.

Inside a typical church

<u>Traditional</u> Roman Catholic, Orthodox and Anglican churches are often very similar in <u>layout</u>.

① ALTAR

The most important place in the church — it is where the <u>Eucharist</u> (Mass or Holy Communion) takes place.

② SANCTUARY

A raised <u>platform</u> where the most <u>important</u> parts of the service take place.

③ PULPIT

A raised box from which the <u>minister</u> gives the <u>sermon</u>.

④ LECTERN

A stand for the <u>church Bible</u> — often in the shape of an eagle.

⑤ FONT

Used to hold <u>water</u> for <u>baptism</u> (see p.80).

⑥ NAVE

The main part of the church where the <u>congregation</u> sits.

Sunday worship in **Church** can take **Many Forms**

1) Most churches have their main service on a <u>Sunday</u> morning. Services usually consist of <u>hymns</u> or <u>songs</u>, <u>Bible readings</u>, <u>prayers</u> and a <u>sermon</u> (talk).

2) The <u>Eucharist</u> (also known as <u>Mass</u> or <u>Holy Communion</u>) is celebrated by most Christian denominations. It's a <u>re-enactment</u> of Jesus's <u>last meal</u> before his crucifixion. Worshippers receive <u>bread</u> and <u>wine</u> which symbolise Jesus's <u>body</u> and <u>blood</u>.

3) Services are normally <u>led</u> by a <u>priest</u> or <u>minister</u>.

4) Men, women and children can <u>sit together</u> in church. Worshippers are usually expected to be <u>quiet</u> during the <u>prayers</u> and to <u>listen respectfully</u> to the <u>sermon</u>.

5) Pentecostals, House Churches and some other denominations may have <u>spontaneous</u>, <u>charismatic</u> worship (lifting their hands, dancing, etc.).

Church services come in a variety of shapes and sizes

Church services can differ depending on which denomination you're talking about. Have a go at familiarising yourself with the names of some of the main features of a traditional church.

Churches — Christianity

Many parts of a church building involve symbolism. A symbol is a thing or word which indicates another meaning.

Religious **Architecture** and **Art** is often **Symbolic**

1) Large cathedrals were historically built at the centre of a community to represent God's kingship on Earth. Inside, the focus of attention is towards the altar.

2) Orthodox and many Anglican and Roman Catholic churches are in the shape of a cross, symbolising the crucifixion. Orthodox churches also have a dome on top to symbolise the nearness of Heaven.

3) Free Churches (e.g. Baptists) meet in simple halls where the pulpit is the focus of attention. This shows the importance of preaching from the Bible.

4) Icons are paintings found in Orthodox churches. They're used to represent the presence of saints or other holy figures, like Jesus or Mary. They're also used to help worshippers pray.

5) Many churches and cathedrals have beautiful stained-glass windows which depict Bible stories and aim to create a sense of awe.

Church **Music** is often used during **Services**

1) Music is an important part of worship in all Christian churches. Handel's 'Messiah' and Mozart's 'Requiem Mass' are famous works composed for worship.

2) Hymns and songs are often based on passages from the Bible.

3) Many different musical instruments are used in worship — from organs to brass bands and electric guitars. The music used can be solemn and dignified or loud and lively, depending on the type of church. Choirs lead the singing in many churches.

4) Dancing is common in Charismatic and Pentecostal churches — it's seen as a sign of the presence of the Holy Spirit.

Churches are often **Open** to the **Community**

1) Lots of Christians believe that churches should be used for much more than Sunday worship.

2) Youth groups are often run by churches to give young people a safe place to have fun. There are often similar groups run for parents with young children and for elderly people.

3) Many churches are open during the week for private prayer and offer cheap or free meals to members of the community, particularly those who are poor and struggle to afford food.

4) Some churches are even open overnight so that homeless people have a place to sleep.

Christian worship is packed full of symbolism

Try to remember the symbols present in Christian worship and what they mean. Many churches aren't just open on a Sunday morning, and they play a big role in their communities.

Synagogues — Judaism

A Jewish place of worship is called a <u>synagogue</u>.

*It's not what's on the **Outside** that matters...*

1) There are no rules stating what a synagogue should look like on the <u>outside</u> — they can be plain, traditional or very modern.

2) Some synagogues have symbols on the walls outside, such as a <u>menorah</u> (a seven-branched candlestick — different from the nine-branched menorah used at Hanukkah on p.61) or a <u>Star of David</u> (see p.36).

*...it's what's on the **Inside** that's important*

The layout of the synagogue's <u>Prayer Hall</u> commemorates some aspects of the ancient <u>Temple</u> in <u>Jerusalem</u>, which was the <u>centre</u> of <u>Jewish worship</u> before it was destroyed in 70 CE (see p.115). All synagogues share the following <u>four features</u>:

① <u>Aron Kodesh</u> (the <u>Ark</u>) — a large <u>cupboard</u> or <u>alcove</u> with doors or a screen. It holds the Torah (see p.44-45) and is set on the wall facing Jerusalem.

② <u>Sefer Torah</u> (Scroll of the Torah) — parchment <u>scroll</u>. It must be <u>handwritten</u> by a <u>sofer</u> (scribe), and is usually decorated. It's kept inside the Ark.

③ <u>Ner Tamid</u> (Perpetual Light) — above the ark is a <u>light</u> which <u>never</u> goes out. It represents the menorah which was always alight in the ancient <u>Temple</u>.

④ <u>Bimah</u> or <u>Almemar</u> — a raised <u>platform</u> with a reading desk, normally in the centre of the hall.

Some synagogues also have a <u>pulpit</u> and a copy of the <u>Ten Commandments</u> above the Ark.

*Shabbat (Sabbath) is celebrated in the **Synagogue***

The <u>Sabbath</u> is a day of <u>rest</u> which commemorates the <u>7th Day of Creation</u>, when G-d rested after creating the Universe. There are three separate <u>services</u> in the synagogue on the Sabbath:

FRIDAY EVENING — Shabbat is welcomed with singing, as if it were a <u>queen</u> or a <u>bride</u>. No instruments are used, in memory of the destruction of the Temple.

SATURDAY MORNING — The <u>main</u> service of the week. The <u>rabbi</u> (teacher) will read from the Torah and give a sermon.

SATURDAY AFTERNOON — This service includes a reading from the <u>Torah</u>, and three special <u>prayers</u>.

Jews go to the synagogue to celebrate Shabbat

Shabbat is the Jewish day of rest — it begins on Friday evening and ends on Saturday evening. There are some tricky terms on this page, so make sure you read it carefully.

Synagogues — Judaism

The synagogue is primarily a place of prayer, but it is also used for celebrations and education.

Jews must Cover their Heads in the Synagogue

1) Everyone except young, unmarried women must wear a hat in the synagogue to show respect for G-d. Most men wear a kippah, which is a small round cap.

2) Adult men often wear a prayer shawl called a tallit whilst attending morning prayers.

3) In Orthodox synagogues, men and women must sit separately to ensure that they are focused on G-d and not on each other. In Reform synagogues, men and women sit together.

Worship in a synagogue is Prayerful

1) Services in a synagogue are led by rabbis or by members of the congregation. Synagogues often have a cantor — a singer specially trained in leading prayers.

2) The reciting of prayers often forms the majority of a service at a synagogue. The atmosphere is respectful and reflective, and singing isn't normally accompanied by instruments.

The Synagogue is important for the Community

1) The synagogue is used for important events, e.g. Bar Mitzvah and Bat Mitzvah ceremonies (see p.83), as well as Jewish weddings and funerals.

2) Jews will often live near to their synagogue, placing it at the centre of their community.

3) Children and adults attend the synagogue for Jewish teaching and education. Children often go to Hebrew lessons so that they can read the Tenakh in its original language.

Jews have No Pictures of G-d

There are two reasons why Jewish art never tries to picture G-d.
1) No one knows what he looks like.
2) The 2nd Commandment forbids it as idolatry (worshipping anything other than G-d).

To avoid idolatry, no images of people are allowed in synagogues either, as people are made in the image of G-d. This also means that sculptures are forbidden.

"You shall not make for yourself an image in the form of anything in heaven above or on the earth beneath..." Exodus 20:4 NIV

Why 'G-d'?

In Deuteronomy 12:1-4, G-d tells the Jews to wipe out the names of the gods they find written in the sacred places of other nations in Israel, but he also warns them not to do the same to him. To avoid risking erasing the name of G-d, Jews never write it out fully.

Jews are careful to respect G-d in the synagogue

Worship in the synagogue varies depending on the individual synagogue and the type of service, but it usually involves periods of recited prayer as well as readings from the Torah.

Mosques — Islam

A <u>mosque</u> is more than a place of worship — it's also the centre of the <u>community</u>.

A **Mosque** is the Muslim house of prayer

1) The <u>Prophet Muhammad</u> said that any <u>clean</u> place could be used for worship.

2) Some mosques are extremely <u>simple</u>, others are very <u>grand</u>. Most have a <u>dome</u> on top to represent the Universe.

3) Most mosques have at least one <u>minaret</u>. This is a tall tower from where a <u>male official</u> from the mosque calls people to <u>pray</u>. The man who does this is called the <u>muezzin</u>.

In countries where Muslims are in a minority, the <u>adhan</u> (call to prayer) is usually broadcast by <u>radio</u>, rather than being called from the top of the minaret.

Mosques are often **Beautifully Decorated**

'Muhammad'

'Allah'

1) Beautiful <u>mosaic tiles</u> often decorate the <u>inside</u> and <u>outside</u> of a mosque.

2) There are no pictures or statues in a mosque. No one is allowed to draw <u>Muhammad</u> or <u>Allah</u>, and images of other <u>living things</u> are usually banned, to avoid <u>idolatry</u> (see p.71).

3) Instead, richly coloured Arabic <u>calligraphy</u> (writing) is used to <u>decorate</u> the walls with words from the Qur'an and the names of Allah and the Prophet Muhammad.

4) There is very <u>little furniture</u> in a mosque. There are no seats, as Muslims use <u>prayer mats</u> when they pray, but there is often a <u>rich carpet</u>.

5) Some mosques have a <u>minbar</u> (pulpit) from which the <u>imam</u> (a respected person) will lead prayers and preach — especially on Fridays.

The mosque is an important place for Muslims

The mosque is at the centre of an Islamic community, being a place of prayer and of study. Friday is the most important day of the week at the mosque, when the main service is held.

Mosques — Islam

A mosque is a place of <u>learning</u> and <u>prayer</u> for the Muslim community.

Muslims must **Wash** before they **Pray**

1) People must take off their <u>shoes</u> when they enter the mosque, to keep it <u>clean</u> for prayer.
2) Every mosque has a place for Muslims to <u>wash</u> before they pray.
3) Each person must wash their <u>hands</u>, <u>mouth</u>, <u>face</u>, <u>forearms</u> and <u>feet</u> — this is known as <u>wudu</u> — it symbolises a spiritual <u>cleansing</u> so that they are ready to come before Allah.
4) Muslims face in the direction of <u>Makkah</u> (the birthplace of <u>Muhammad</u> and the most holy place in Islam) when they pray. Each mosque has a wall which faces towards Makkah, with a <u>mihrab</u> (a hollow space) in that wall so that worshippers know which it is.

> For more on <u>Makkah</u> and its importance to Muslims, see p.113.

5) It is important to wear <u>respectable</u>, <u>modest clothing</u> when attending a mosque. <u>Women</u> must <u>cover</u> their <u>heads</u>, sometimes with a <u>hijab</u> (a veil which covers the head and chest). All Muslims are expected to wear their <u>best clothes</u> when they attend <u>Friday prayers</u>.
6) <u>Loud talking</u> is <u>forbidden</u> inside the mosque so that people praying aren't <u>distracted</u>.

Imams lead **Services** at the mosque

1) The main service in the mosque is on <u>Friday</u>, at <u>noon</u>. All <u>males</u> are expected to attend unless they are ill or travelling.
2) At the service, the <u>imam</u> gives a <u>sermon</u> and then <u>leads</u> worshippers in <u>prayer</u>. He will often <u>recite verses</u> from the Qur'an during the prayers.
3) <u>Women</u> do not have to attend the mosque, but if they do, they must pray in a <u>separate</u> section of the mosque, usually at the back.
4) Women <u>don't</u> lead prayers in the mosque if a man is available, but they may lead prayers for other <u>women and children</u>.

The mosque is a **Place** of **Learning**

1) Apart from prayer, a mosque is used as a <u>madrasah</u> (a mosque school) where Muslims learn the <u>general principles</u> of Islam and how to carry out <u>Muslim practices</u>.
2) Muslims may also spend time in the mosque, <u>learning</u> and <u>reciting</u> the <u>Qur'an</u>.
3) Mosques also provide a place for Muslims to <u>meet together</u>, to <u>support</u> each other and to <u>discuss</u> any <u>problems</u> or issues there might be in the <u>community</u>.

Allah is the focus of Muslim worship

There's plenty to learn on these pages, including quite a few words that are probably new to you. Mosques are very important to Muslims — they're at the centre of Islamic communities.

Gurdwaras — Sikhism

A gurdwara is a place where Sikhs can go to worship Waheguru (God).

Any building Containing the Sikh Scriptures can be a Gurdwara

1) Sikhs come together to worship in a gurdwara. 'Gurdwara' literally means 'gateway to Waheguru'.

2) Therefore, worshipping at the gurdwara puts Sikhs on the path towards enlightenment (see p.22).

3) Although Sikhs come to a gurdwara to worship Waheguru, they also believe that he is present everywhere.

4) The Sikh holy book, the Guru Granth Sahib (see p.48), contains the gurus' words, so any building which contains it can be considered a gurdwara.

Everyone is Welcome to enter a gurdwara

1) A gurdwara has four entrances — the Door of Peace, the Door of Livelihood, the Door of Learning and the Door of Grace.

2) This symbolises that people from the four points of the compass and the four castes (see p.21) are all welcome to enter the gurdwara. Everyone is welcome, regardless of their religion or background.

3) The Sikh flag (the Nishan Sahib) is visible outside the gurdwara.

4) There is also always a light on to show that anyone can enter the gurdwara at any time.

5) The main hall of a gurdwara is called a darbar — this is where believers gather to pray or take part in a service.

6) There are usually no decorations, religious pictures or statues present in the gurdwara because Sikhs only worship God, and they don't believe that God has a physical form. However, some gurdwaras have pictures of Guru Nanak and the other gurus on the walls.

A Gurdwara is a place for all the Community

1) Every gurdwara has a kitchen (a langar) attached to it. It provides a free, simple meal for anyone who would like one — whatever their religion. The food is vegetarian so that most visitors can eat it.

2) Gurdwaras sometimes have libraries or schools attached to them to aid religious teaching.

3) There is also sometimes a room where Sikhs can go to take part in charity work to help the community.

A gurdwara is simply decorated

Gurdwaras might not be full of fancy decorations and pictures, but many of their features emphasise the fact that everyone is welcome — the four entrances, langar and constant light.

Gurdwaras — Sikhism

There are traditional <u>customs</u> that Sikhs follow when they visit the <u>gurdwara</u>.

The **Guru Granth Sahib** is treated with **Great Respect**

1) The <u>Guru Granth Sahib</u> is the Sikh holy book. It is the most important thing in a gurdwara — it is <u>respected</u> in the same way as a human guru would be treated.

2) At night, the Guru Granth Sahib is kept in a <u>special room</u> of its own, and is then carried to the <u>darbar</u> (main hall) at the start of worship in the morning.

3) The book is placed on a <u>takhat</u> (a raised platform that literally means "throne") at the front of the hall. There is a canopy above the book which is called a <u>chanani</u>.

4) When the Guru Granth Sahib is not being used, it is <u>covered</u> with an <u>expensive cloth</u>.

5) When Sikhs first enter the gurdwara, they <u>bow</u> to the Guru Granth Sahib to show their <u>respect</u> for the book's content.

6) <u>Donations</u> are also placed in front of the book — <u>money</u>, <u>food</u> or <u>flowers</u> are typical offerings. Donations are used to run the gurdwara and <u>langar</u>.

Sikhs **Behave Respectfully** inside the **Gurdwara**

1) Before entering the gurdwara, all visitors must <u>remove their shoes</u> and <u>cover their heads</u>.

2) Inside the gurdwara, worshippers sit on the <u>floor</u> — this symbolises that everyone is low and <u>humble</u> compared to Waheguru, and that everyone is of <u>equal status</u>. Men and women usually sit <u>separately</u>, and at an <u>equal distance</u> from the Guru Granth Sahib to show their <u>equality</u>.

3) As a mark of respect, Sikhs point their <u>feet</u> away from the Guru Granth Sahib.

4) Visitors walk <u>clockwise</u> around the gurdwara to keep the <u>energy</u> flowing in the right direction around the Guru Granth Sahib.

Sikh **Festivals** are usually **Celebrated** inside the gurdwara

1) Many Sikh ceremonies, including <u>marriage</u> services and <u>funerals</u>, are held at the gurdwara.

2) <u>Any</u> Sikh can lead a prayer service. There are no ordained priests, but there is a <u>Granthi</u> who is <u>trained</u> to look after, and read from, the <u>Guru Granth Sahib</u>.

3) <u>Kirtan</u> (hymn-singing) is an essential part of Sikh worship. Hymns from the Guru Granth Sahib are accompanied by <u>musical instruments</u>.

4) A <u>blessed</u> sweet food called <u>karah parshad</u> is served to all visitors to the gurdwara. It should be taken with <u>cupped hands</u> while sitting because it is seen as a <u>gift</u> from Waheguru.

5) The karah parshad is made of <u>equal</u> amounts of <u>sugar</u>, <u>butter</u> and <u>flour</u>, which symbolise equality between <u>men</u> and <u>women</u>. It is also served in equal portions.

The Guru Granth Sahib is the focal point in the gurdwara

You should have an idea of what it's like inside a gurdwara now. There are quite a few Sikh customs to learn on these pages — gurdwaras serve a lot of purposes for Sikhs.

Temples — Buddhism

Buddhists can worship anywhere, but many choose to visit a temple to <u>think</u>, <u>meditate</u> or <u>pray</u>.

Buddhists Visit the temple Whenever they can

1) A Buddhist temple is a <u>peaceful</u> place for people to <u>reflect</u>, <u>meditate</u> and <u>make offerings</u>.

2) There is no set time or day when Buddhists visit the temple — they go <u>whenever</u> they want. But it's also common for Buddhists to visit the temple to mark the <u>full moon</u> — many important Buddhist events are believed to have happened on the day of a full moon, especially the Buddha's <u>enlightenment</u> (see p.19).

3) Buddhist temples come in <u>different</u> shapes and sizes. One type of temple is a <u>stupa</u>, where the main body of the temple is a <u>mound</u> shape.

4) A <u>pagoda</u> — a <u>tiered</u> tower commonly found in <u>Japan</u> and <u>China</u> — is another typical style of Buddhist temple.

5) Temples often contain Buddhist <u>relics</u> (<u>ancient artefacts</u>, e.g. the <u>ashes</u> of Buddhist monks or copies of Buddhist <u>scriptures</u>).

Stupas often symbolise the Five Elements

1) The symbolisation of <u>stupa</u> temples can vary, but the representation of the <u>five elements</u> (earth, water, fire, air and space) is popular in many.

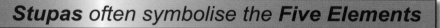

- The square <u>base</u> of the temple represents <u>earth</u>, symbolising <u>durability</u>.
- <u>Water</u> is represented by the round <u>dome</u> of the stupa.
- The <u>canopy</u> of the stupa represents <u>air</u>, which symbolises <u>openness</u>.
- <u>Fire</u> is represented by the <u>cone</u> shape and symbolises <u>energy</u> and <u>warmth</u>.
- <u>Space</u> is represented by the <u>pinnacle</u> at the top of the building.

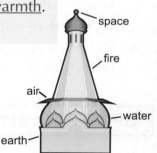

space
fire
air
water
earth

2) Buddhist temples are often elaborately <u>decorated</u> with carvings, gold and precious stones.

3) There are statues and/or images of the <u>Buddha</u> in all temples, and in other <u>shrines</u>. People often make <u>offerings</u> to these statues or images in <u>honour</u> of the Buddha.

4) Temples are usually decorated with <u>candles</u>, <u>flowers</u> and <u>images</u> of the Buddha and his enlightenment (see p.19), and there's often <u>incense</u> burning.

Buddhists Worship by Chanting

1) Buddhists remove their <u>shoes</u> before entering the temple, as a mark of respect for the Buddha.

2) Worshippers usually <u>sit</u> on the floor facing the statue or picture of the Buddha and <u>chant</u> religious texts, pray or meditate.

3) Believers also recite <u>mantras</u> — these are words or short phrases which are <u>repeated</u> over and over. Many Buddhists use <u>prayer beads</u> to keep track of how many times they've recited a mantra.

The Buddhist temple is a place for reflection

Buddhist temples are not always the same, but they often have things in common. Try to learn a few of the typical characteristics of stupas — and why those features are important.

Temples — Hinduism

A Hindu temple is called a <u>mandir</u> — each mandir is dedicated to one or more <u>deities</u> (gods).

Hindus Don't have to Worship in a Mandir

1) Hinduism places a lot of emphasis on the <u>family</u> unit — children are taught about religion at home. Most of their <u>puja</u> (worship) is done at <u>home</u>, in private, at a small shrine.

2) However, many Hindus also choose to visit a <u>mandir</u> to offer prayers to one or more deities (gods).

3) Mandirs are often located near important geographical features such as <u>caves</u>, <u>hills</u> or <u>waterfalls</u> to make it easier for worshippers to focus. Some Hindus also believe that the gods <u>play</u> near these geographical features, so worshipping there allows them to feel <u>closer</u> to their gods.

4) Many mandirs are <u>dedicated</u> to one particular <u>deity</u>, but others are dedicated to groups of associated deities. There are <u>statues</u> or images of the chosen deities (called <u>murtis</u>) inside the mandir (see p.35 for the Hindu deities).

The Murtis are kept in the Garbhagriha

1) The <u>features</u> of a Hindu temple vary, but there is often a <u>garbhagriha</u> (or inner sanctuary).

2) This is where the main <u>murtis</u> are kept — they are placed on a stone <u>pedestal</u> in an ornately decorated <u>altar</u>.

3) There is also a <u>puja tray</u> where <u>offerings</u> to the deity are placed.

4) There are usually flowers and an <u>oil lamp</u> in the altar, and curtains are hung over the altar's entrance.

5) The <u>main hall</u> (<u>mandapa</u>) in larger temples, where believers <u>pray</u>, <u>meditate</u> and watch the priests perform <u>rituals</u>, is usually <u>decorated</u> with images of the gods (murtis).

Hindus Pray in front of the Murtis

1) Some worshippers ring the <u>ghanta</u> (bell) to mark their <u>arrival</u> at the temple.

2) They remove their <u>shoes</u> before entering the mandir, and once inside, they keep <u>one hand cupped inside the other</u> on their laps as a sign of respect.

3) Hindus pray to the murtis by reciting <u>mantras</u> (see p.76) and verses from the sacred texts, such as the <u>Bhagavad Gita</u>. Then they <u>bow</u> in front of the deity, often <u>lying</u> flat on the floor.

4) Next, worshippers will make an <u>offering</u>. The offering is often something that represents the <u>natural</u> world, like flowers or fruit.

5) Sometimes the priest might offer a small tray of five <u>candles</u>, or a five-wick candle, to the worshippers, who touch the <u>flames</u> with their hand and then touch their hand to their forehead. This is called <u>Aarti</u> — it symbolises the receipt of a god's <u>power</u>.

6) Finally, Hindus walk <u>clockwise</u> around the murtis, stopping once on each side to <u>pray</u>. By walking in a clockwise direction, the deities are always on the worshipper's right-hand side — reminding them to stay on the <u>right path</u> in life.

A murti is a symbol of a god — it makes prayer more focused

A mandir is often dedicated to one particular deity. A family usually has a deity who they focus their prayers on at home, too. Remember, most of the time, Hindus worship at home.

Questions

After all those places of worship, it's time to pay a visit to the depths of your mind and see how much information from the section you've managed to remember. Easy questions first...

Warm-up Questions

1) On which day of the week do most Christian church services happen?
2) What must most Jews cover when they enter a synagogue?
3) What does the imam do at a mosque?
4) Briefly describe how Sikhs should behave inside a gurdwara.
5) Why do Buddhists remove their shoes before entering a temple?

Practice Questions

Muscles flexed, blood pumping — time for some meatier questions.

1) Match these features of a traditional church on the left to their functions on the right.
   - a) pulpit
   - b) font
   - c) lectern
   - d) nave
   - e) altar
   - i) where the Eucharist (Mass or Holy Communion) takes place
   - ii) where the congregation sits
   - iii) a stand to hold the Bible
   - iv) where the minister gives the sermon
   - v) holds water for baptism

2) Are these sentences about Jewish worship true or false?
   - a) The Torah is kept in the Aron Kodesh, which faces Makkah.
   - b) The Ner Tamid is only lit when a service is in progress.
   - c) Most synagogues have their main services on Friday mornings.
   - d) The Sefer Torah must be handwritten by a scribe.

3) Copy out and complete this passage, adding the correct words from the list below:

   langar   **peaceful**   **statues**   **stupa**   **murti**   **gurdwara**   **mandir**   **pagoda**

   a) Sikhs worship in a _____. This name can be given to any building that contains the Sikh scriptures. Anyone is welcome to attend, and there's a kitchen called a _____ attached to the building. Sikhs don't believe that God has a physical form, so there are no pictures or _____ in the building.

   b) Buddhist temples are usually _____ places which Buddhists visit whenever they want. There are many different styles of temple, including the _____, which has a mound-like shape, and the _____, which is a tiered tower.

   c) A Hindu temple is known as a _____. Many Hindus mainly worship at home, but attend a temple to offer special prayers to the deities (gods). Temples are often dedicated to one particular deity, and there's normally a statue or _____ of that deity there.

Section Four — Summary Questions

Here are some harder questions that will require a bit more thought. Remember that it's best to have a go at them first, then check back through the section for some help if you need it. All the answers you'll need are on the pages you've just read.

1) What is the Eucharist (Mass or Holy Communion) a re-enactment of?

2) Baptist churches are often very plainly decorated. Explain why this is.

3) Give an example of how music is used in Christian worship.

4) Give two examples of ways in which a church can help the community.

5) Why would a man not sit next to his wife in an Orthodox synagogue?

6) Describe a typical service at a synagogue.

7) Explain why some Jews write 'G-d' instead of 'God'.

8) How is the inside of a mosque normally decorated?

9) Why are there very few chairs in a mosque?

10) Name four parts of the body that Muslims must wash before they pray.
    Explain why they must do this.

11) What are all male Muslims expected to do at noon on a Friday?
    Are there any exceptions to this rule?

12) How many entrances are there to a gurdwara? What does this number symbolise?

13) What is the Nishan Sahib? Where could you see it at a gurdwara?

14) Give three ways in which the Guru Granth Sahib is treated with respect.

15) Which sweet food is served to all visitors at a gurdwara during some Sikh festivals?
    How should they receive it?

16) Why do Buddhists often visit temples during a full moon?

17) List the five elements that are often represented in a Buddhist stupa.

18) What are mantras? What do some Buddhists use to help them with their mantras?

19) Why might you be more likely to find a mandir in the countryside than in a city?

20) Name three things which take place in the mandapa of a mandir.

21) Give an example of something that a Hindu may present as an offering at a mandir.

22) "Places of worship are much more than fancy buildings."
    Discuss this statement, including different points of view, as well as your viewpoint.
    You should refer to a religion in your answer.

Christian Birth Ceremonies

Christians like to <u>welcome</u> new babies into their community — they can do this with a <u>baptism</u> or a <u>dedication</u>.

Infant Baptism cleanses the baby from Original Sin

1) Some Christians <u>baptise</u> (or <u>christen</u>) babies to cleanse them from the <u>original sin</u> that every person is born with. They believe this gives them a fresh start in life and makes them a member of God's <u>family</u>.

2) Before the ceremony, parents will choose close friends or family to act as <u>godparents</u> to the child. Godparents should give the child spiritual <u>guidance</u>, so parents will choose people who they hope will be good <u>role models</u>.

3) Parents and godparents <u>promise</u> to bring the child up as a part of the <u>Christian community</u>.

4) A sign of the <u>cross</u> is made on the baby, and <u>holy water</u> is poured <u>three</u> times over the forehead (in the name of the <u>Father</u>, <u>Son</u> and <u>Holy Spirit</u>). Orthodox Christians, however, baptise babies by <u>total immersion</u>.

5) A special <u>candle</u> is lit to symbolise the light of Christ entering the baby's life. The candle may be given to a parent or godparent, to remind them of their <u>duty</u> to the child.

> Original sin is a result of the Fall of man — when Adam and Eve disobeyed God in the Garden of Eden. By disobeying God, they lost their innocence, and so did the rest of humankind.

Some Christians receive a Dedication instead of a baptism

1) Some denominations (e.g. Baptists) believe you <u>shouldn't</u> be baptised until you are old enough to accept Christianity for <u>yourself</u>. In this case the baby is <u>dedicated</u> instead.

2) During a dedication <u>service</u>, the child's parents, family and sometimes the whole congregation <u>promise</u> to help raise the child as part of their community. The idea is to <u>teach</u> them how to live a good Christian life, so that when they are older, they will <u>choose</u> to follow God for themselves.

3) The service is very <u>similar</u> to the infant baptism ceremony, but <u>without</u> baptising the baby with <u>holy water</u>.

Baptism marks the start of a new life

So, at an infant baptism service, parents make a promise to God on the child's behalf, but at a dedication ceremony they promise to help prepare the child to make that decision alone.

Jewish Birth Ceremonies

The <u>birth</u> of a baby is an event to be <u>celebrated</u>, and each religion has its own rituals — this page is about <u>Jewish</u> birth ceremonies.

Jewish baby **Boys** have a **Brit Milah** ceremony

1) <u>Brit Milah</u> is a <u>circumcision</u> ceremony which usually takes place when the boy is <u>eight days</u> old.

2) Most Jewish <u>boys</u> are circumcised — this was the sign of the <u>covenant</u> (deal) which G-d made with <u>Abraham</u> over 3000 years ago, as part of which G-d <u>promised</u> him many descendants.

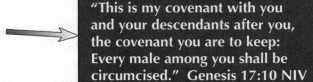

"This is my covenant with you and your descendants after you, the covenant you are to keep: Every male among you shall be circumcised." Genesis 17:10 NIV

3) There are other <u>reasons</u> that circumcision is <u>important</u> to Jews:

- It is a <u>symbol</u> of the boy's <u>bond</u> with G-d which will <u>always</u> be with him.
- The act of circumcision is thought to be a small human <u>input</u> to <u>complete</u> G-d's <u>creation</u>. This reminds Jews that although G-d created the world, humans need to make the final <u>effort</u> for things to be <u>perfect</u>.
- Circumcision is also considered to be more <u>hygienic</u>, and it <u>purifies</u> the organ that is the <u>source of life</u>.

4) Brit Milah often takes place in a <u>synagogue</u>, but it can also be held at <u>home</u>.

5) The circumcision is performed by a <u>mohel</u> (a Jewish person trained to carry out the procedure), while the godfather holds the boy still (the person who fulfils this role is the <u>sandek</u>).

6) Brit Milah is followed by a <u>celebratory</u> meal which includes praying for the boy to grow into a <u>good person</u>.

Any child born to a **Jewish Mother** is considered a **Jew**

1) If a baby's <u>mother</u> is a Jew, then the child is automatically considered part of the <u>Jewish</u> community.

2) Jewish babies are given their <u>names</u> when they attend their first public gathering — the name is kept a <u>secret</u> until then.

3) For a baby <u>boy</u>, their first public event will be their <u>Brit Milah</u>.

4) A baby <u>girl</u> will be named when she attends her first public reading of the Torah at the <u>synagogue</u>.

A baby's name is kept secret until they attend their first gathering

Make sure you remember the term Brit Milah, what happens during the ceremony, and why. Baby girls don't have a traditional ceremony like a Brit Milah, but their birth is still celebrated.

82

Muslim Birth Ceremonies

The <u>first week</u> of a Muslim baby's life is very important — there are a number of simple <u>rituals</u> that the family follow to <u>welcome</u> the child into the world.

*A prayer to **Allah** should be the **First** thing a newborn child hears*

1) When a baby is born, the father whispers the Muslim <u>call to prayer</u> (the adhan — see p.72) in the baby's <u>right</u> ear. <u>Prayer</u> is a key part of the Muslim faith, so babies are introduced to this straight away.

2) A baby's first taste should be of something <u>sweet</u>, so parents will often rub the juice of a date on the baby's gums. This is a tradition passed down from the <u>Prophet Muhammad</u>. Some Muslims believe that it helps the baby's <u>digestive system</u>; others hope it will help the child grow up to be <u>obedient</u> and <u>kind</u>.

*The **Seventh** day is important*

1) The baby's <u>hair</u> is traditionally <u>shaved</u> off once it is seven days old — this shows that the baby is a servant of Allah.

2) The parents then <u>weigh</u> the hair and give the equivalent weight of silver to <u>charity</u>.

3) The child is also <u>named</u> on the seventh day — choosing a good Muslim name is important.

4) Most Muslim boys are <u>circumcised</u>. This may happen on the seventh day too, or at some later time before puberty.

5) <u>Reasons</u> for circumcision include:

- It's seen as a symbol of <u>belonging</u> — it marks their <u>introduction</u> to Islam.
- It's considered to improve <u>cleanliness</u>, which is very important to Muslims, especially during prayer.

*The **Aqiqah** celebration takes place on the **Seventh** day*

1) The <u>aqiqah</u> (or aqeeqah) is a big <u>celebration</u>. It traditionally involves sacrificing <u>sheep</u> or <u>goats</u>, but in the UK people tend to order the meat from the butchers.

2) A large amount of the meat is given to the <u>poor</u>, and the rest is shared with <u>friends</u> and <u>family</u> to celebrate the <u>birth</u> of the child.

3) During the <u>aqiqah</u>, <u>prayers</u> are also said to thank <u>Allah</u> for the baby and to ask him to protect the family.

Allah enters a Muslim baby's life as soon as it's born

For Muslims, religious rituals are important from the moment a baby is born. Make sure you learn the different birth rites discussed on this page, and why they're carried out.

Judaism — Bar/Bat Mitzvah

Coming of age ceremonies are very important for young Jews — read this page to find out more.

Boys have a *Bar Mitzvah* and *Girls* have a *Bat Mitzvah*

1) A Bar Mitzvah is celebrated when a <u>boy</u> reaches <u>13</u> years old, and a Bat Mitzvah when a <u>girl</u> reaches <u>12</u> years old.

2) The ceremony marks a person's <u>passage</u> from a child to an <u>adult</u> — they are now <u>responsible</u> for their own actions.

> The terms Bar/Bat Mitzvah can refer to the <u>person</u> who is coming of age, the <u>ceremony</u>, or the <u>celebration</u> afterwards.

The Bar/Bat Mitzvah **Ceremony** *takes place in a* **Synagogue**

1) A Bar/Bat Mitzvah ceremony <u>varies</u> slightly depending on which strand of Judaism the family follows, but the meaning behind it is the same. There's <u>no ceremony</u> at all for <u>girls</u> in <u>Orthodox</u> Jewish families, but they might have a private celebration.

2) The young person <u>studies</u> the <u>Torah</u> (the Jewish holy book, see p.44-45) to <u>prepare</u> for the ceremony.

3) They will then be involved in the <u>Shabbat service</u> at the synagogue. They might lead some of the <u>prayers</u>, give a <u>speech</u> or read some of the <u>blessings</u>.

4) During the ceremony, the Bar/Bat Mitzvah <u>promises</u> to keep G-d's <u>commandments</u>. This marks the <u>beginning</u> of a life-long religious <u>education</u> and <u>participation</u> in the Jewish community.

5) After the ceremony, the Bar/Bat Mitzvah's family might throw a <u>party</u> to celebrate.

After coming of age, Jews wear a **Tallit** *and* **Tefillin**

1) When a young person comes of age, they are treated as an <u>adult</u>, so they can wear a <u>tallit</u> and a <u>tefillin</u> while praying.

2) The <u>tallit</u> is a large <u>shawl</u> with tied strings at each of the four corners. The strings are tied in a particular pattern to remind Jews of their <u>duty</u> to G-d.

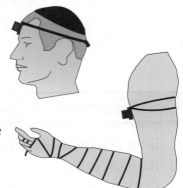

3) The <u>tefillin</u> consists of two black leather <u>boxes</u> which are attached to the wearer with long straps. One box is worn on the upper arm, and the other box is worn on the forehead. Inside the boxes are handwritten <u>verses</u> from the Torah. Wearing the tefillin reminds Jews to serve G-d with both <u>head</u> and <u>heart</u>.

Once a Bar/Bat Mitzvah, a Jew is responsible for their own actions

A Bar or Bat Mitzvah is a very important time for a Jew — it's when they become an adult and gain religious responsibilities. Take responsibility too, and learn the key points from this page.

Christianity — Confirmation and Adult Baptism

Adult baptism and confirmation are two ways that people can show their <u>faith</u> in God.

Baptism *Symbolises the start of a* New Life

1) <u>Adults</u> can be baptised if they haven't already been baptised as babies.

2) Some denominations baptise <u>infants</u>. Others believe the person should be an <u>adult</u>, so they can decide for themselves (see p.80).

3) During most adult baptism services, the person is immersed in <u>water</u> to symbolise the washing away of <u>sins</u>.

4) The believer promises to follow the teachings of <u>Christianity</u> and begins a <u>new life</u> as part of the Church.

Confirmation *helps strengthen a person's* Faith

1) Denominations which practise <u>infant baptism</u> have a ceremony of <u>confirmation</u> when the child comes of age.

2) In this ceremony, the person <u>renews the promises</u> made on their behalf at their <u>baptism</u>.

3) In Roman Catholic confirmations, the bishop anoints the believer's forehead with holy oil called <u>chrism</u>.

4) Roman Catholics may get confirmed when they're considered old enough to <u>understand</u> what it means. This can be from the age of seven, but it is frequently done later — they have to show that they <u>understand</u> their faith, usually by attending a course of <u>religious instruction</u>.

5) Some other Christian denominations prefer to <u>wait</u> until the child is in their <u>teens</u>, and can fully understand their faith, before carrying out the confirmation ceremony.

6) Denominations which practise only <u>adult baptism</u> usually <u>do not</u> have a confirmation ceremony.

Confirmation *is a step further than* Baptism

1) Both ceremonies are opportunities for a Christian to show their <u>faith</u> in God.

2) Baptism is a way of <u>welcoming</u> somebody to the Church, whereas a confirmation <u>demonstrates</u> the beliefs of somebody who is already a member.

A confirmation confirms the promises made at a baptism

Think about why a person might want to take part in either of these rites of passage. The key point to remember is that they're making a promise to God in front of the rest of the Church.

Christian Death Rites

Every religion has a special way of dealing with the dead. A funeral is a ceremony carried out when a person has died — this page is on Christian funerals.

Christian Funerals are Sad, but with a note of Hope

1) Funeral services vary according to denomination, but all Christian funerals contain a note of hope because Christians believe in God's promises of eternal life in Heaven (see p.138).

2) It doesn't matter whether the body's buried or cremated (burned) — Christians believe they will be given new spiritual bodies after death.

3) The coffin is carried into the church, and the priest often gives a short sermon about Christian belief in life after death, and may also talk about the life of the person who has died.

4) There are prayers for the bereaved (those close to the person who's died), and members of the congregation will express their sympathy for the family and close friends of the deceased.

Funeral Customs help Support the Bereaved

1) Christian funeral services focus on hope of eternal life. The bereaved are encouraged to believe that one day they will be reunited with the deceased (dead person).

2) In the days following the funeral, family and friends often try to contact those who were closest to the deceased, and encourage them to talk through their grief.

3) Usually the priest or minister will also try to visit, and may offer counselling, or suggest someone who can.

4) There are several stages to the process of mourning, and it can help to talk to someone who understands this.

Mourning is a deep sorrow for someone who has died. During a period of mourning, loved ones say special prayers for the deceased, remember their lives and go without pleasures (e.g. music, bright colours, sex). At the end of that period, mourners try to move on with their lives.

God's promise of eternal life can comfort grieving Christians

Funerals and death aren't the happiest of subjects to talk about, so these few pages are a bit gloomy. But belief in life after death adds an element of hope to Christian funerals.

Jewish Death Rites

Judaism has <u>many rituals</u> surrounding death — they're mainly to help the <u>bereaved</u> cope.

Jews *Stay* with *Loved Ones* while they *Die*

1) Jewish families <u>gather together</u> to be near a loved one who is dying.

2) The dying person should spend his or her last moments <u>confessing</u> sins and reciting the <u>Shema</u> (see p.50).

3) After the death, members of an Orthodox family will make a small <u>tear</u> in their clothing as a symbol of <u>grief</u>. This is less common in Reform Judaism.

4) The dead person must not be left alone, and must be <u>buried</u> (not cremated) as soon as possible, preferably within <u>24 hours</u>. Reform Jews often allow longer, so that the family has more time to organise the funeral.

A Jewish funeral *Service* should be *Simple*

1) Simplicity is important in a Jewish funeral — in death, rich and poor are <u>equal</u>. The body is <u>ritually bathed</u>, wrapped in a plain linen <u>shroud</u>, and placed in a plain, unpolished, wooden <u>coffin</u>.

2) The funeral service is held at a <u>synagogue</u>, but the funeral <u>procession</u> traditionally makes several ceremonial <u>stops</u> along the way. This is meant to symbolise the <u>difficulty</u> that mourners have in letting go of the deceased.

3) For some Jews, it is customary to recite sections of <u>psalms 90 and 91</u> at each stop. Psalm 90 is a <u>blessing</u> written by Moses, and psalm 91 is known as the psalm of <u>protection</u>.

4) At the service, G-d is praised for <u>giving</u> life and for <u>taking</u> it away. The rabbi might also make a short speech about the deceased.

Mourning *continues* for *Thirty Days* after death

1) The first week after the funeral is called <u>shiva</u> (seven). The immediate family stay at home and are <u>visited</u> by relatives and friends, who pray with them and offer comfort.

2) The first month after the funeral is called <u>sheloshim</u> (thirty). During this time, life returns <u>gradually</u> to normal, and male mourners go to the synagogue to recite the <u>kaddish</u> — a Jewish mourning prayer.

3) Anyone who has lost a <u>parent</u> remains in mourning for a whole <u>year</u>. This extra mourning time gives children the opportunity to <u>consider</u> all that their parents did for them and to come to terms with the <u>loss</u>.

Judaism teaches that, in death, all are equal

So, the funeral of a Jewish king would follow the same format as any other Jew. There are no elaborate coffins or fancy floral displays — simplicity is key. Then comes the mourning period.

Muslim Death Rites

Muslims <u>prepare</u> a person for the <u>next life</u> by following certain rituals.

'Allah' should be the **Last Word** a Muslim hears

A Muslim hopes <u>not</u> to die <u>alone</u>, but with relatives and friends around, who will:

- Keep them <u>company</u> and look after them.
- Ensure last-minute business is settled. A dying Muslim should focus on <u>Allah</u> without being <u>distracted</u> by other things.
- <u>Pray</u> and <u>recite</u> 'There is no god but Allah' in Arabic, so that the person can <u>concentrate</u> on the name of God. Allah should be the <u>last</u> word a Muslim hears.

Bodies are **Buried** facing **Makkah**

1) After a person has died, the body is <u>washed</u>, as a sign of respect.
2) The body is then <u>wrapped</u> in a clean white shroud and buried as soon as possible.
3) <u>Janazah</u> prayers (funeral prayers) are said, praying that the dead person may be judged <u>mercifully</u> and gain a place in <u>Paradise</u> (see p.90).
4) The body is <u>buried</u> in a simple grave, lying on its <u>right side</u> with the face towards <u>Makkah</u>.
5) Muslims prefer to bury their dead <u>without a coffin</u> — but this is not allowed in the UK.
6) Muslims bury their dead rather than cremating them, because they believe that the body will be physically <u>resurrected</u> (brought back to life) on the Day of Judgement — so the person still needs it.
7) A period of <u>mourning</u> is kept for <u>three days</u>, finishing with Qur'an reading and prayers for the dead person. Some Muslims do this after 40 days as well.

Muslims are buried, not cremated

As Muslims pass from this world, they should be thinking of Allah — they will soon be judged on how they have lived. If they've pleased Allah they will be rewarded with life in Paradise.

Life After Death: Christianity

What people believe will happen to them in death can <u>influence</u> the way they live their lives.

Christian teaching — *Heaven* and *Hell*

1) Christianity teaches that death is <u>not the end</u> — the dead person <u>lives on</u> in another place.

2) Traditional Christians believe that God will judge you, and you'll go either to <u>Heaven</u> or <u>Hell</u>.

Heaven

Heaven is not closely described, but is thought of as a place of <u>beauty</u> and <u>serenity</u> for those who pass the test of <u>judgement</u>.

Hell

Hell is portrayed as a place of <u>torment</u> and <u>pain</u> — the final destination of those who have led <u>bad</u> lives.

3) However, not all Christians believe that these are <u>real</u> places — many Christians see Heaven and Hell as <u>states of mind</u>. In Heaven you'll be <u>happy</u> and know God — in Hell you'll be <u>unable</u> to know God's love.

4) Roman Catholics also believe in an intermediate place called <u>Purgatory</u>. Here sins are <u>punished</u> before the dead person is able to move on to <u>Heaven</u>. This concept isn't in the Bible, so Protestants reject it.

5) The fear of <u>punishment</u> or promise of <u>reward</u> in the afterlife <u>encourages</u> believers to live good lives.

Jesus promised *Eternal Life* to his *Followers*

This is how the Christian Church sees death and resurrection:

1) Human beings <u>sin</u> (disobey God), so they're not <u>fit</u> to be accepted into Heaven.

2) But Jesus's death <u>redeemed</u> humankind so that they can be accepted. <u>Repentance</u> (being sorry for past sins) and <u>faith</u> (trust in God) enable a person to <u>enter Heaven</u>.

> "I am the resurrection and the life. The one who believes in me will live, even though they die; and whoever lives by believing in me will never die." John 11:25-26 NIV

Many Christians believe in Heaven and Hell

A future in Heaven encourages Christians to follow the Bible's teachings and also helps them to live good lives. They are grateful to Jesus for dying to make an afterlife in Heaven possible.

Life After Death: Judaism

<u>Jews</u> also have some beliefs about what happens after <u>death</u>.

The dead will be **Resurrected** in the **World to Come**

1) Jewish teachings mainly focus on how to live <u>now</u> — a person's <u>duties</u> to G-d and other people. According to the Torah, rewards for obeying G-d, and punishments for 'breaking the covenant', are sent in <u>this world</u> (Leviticus 26:3-17 NIV). But Jews still believe that a dead person lives on <u>forever</u>.

2) Jews believe that the <u>Messiah</u>, a great future leader, will bring an era of <u>perfect peace</u> and <u>prosperity</u> called the <u>World to Come</u> (or <u>messianic age</u>). (Jews don't believe Jesus was the Messiah.)

3) It's believed that the <u>righteous</u> dead (both Jews and non-Jews) will be <u>resurrected</u> to share in this peace. But the <u>wicked</u> dead won't be able to enjoy the World to Come — instead they will be <u>punished</u>.

> "Multitudes who sleep in the dust of the earth will awake: some to everlasting life, others to shame and everlasting contempt."
> Daniel 12:2 NIV

4) Orthodox Jews believe that the <u>physical body</u> will be resurrected. Because of this, <u>cutting up</u> dead bodies to find the cause of death (autopsy) is frowned upon, and <u>cremation</u> is <u>forbidden</u>.

5) Reform Jews believe that the body is only needed during this life, and <u>reject</u> the idea of physical resurrection. So Reform Jews accept cremation and autopsies.

Modern Judaism teaches about **Gan Eden** and **Gehinnom**

1) Modern Jews believe in an afterlife spent in places called <u>Gan Eden</u> ("Garden of Eden" or Paradise) and <u>Gehinnom</u> (a bit like Purgatory, see p.88).

2) Some see Gan Eden as a <u>physical place</u> of grand banquets and sunshine. But others have a more <u>spiritual</u> view of it — as a <u>closeness to G-d</u>.

3) Similarly, there are different views of Gehinnom — a place of fire and physical <u>pain</u>, or a chance to see <u>missed</u> <u>opportunities</u> and the <u>harm</u> a person caused in life.

4) Only if you've lived a <u>blameless life</u> will you be sent straight to Gan Eden when you die.

5) Most souls are sent to Gehinnom for a period of <u>punishment</u> and <u>purification</u> first, which lasts up to <u>12 months</u>, before ascending to Gan Eden. Only the <u>truly wicked</u> never reach Paradise.

6) This means that your behaviour <u>now</u> determines what kind of <u>afterlife</u> you receive. So <u>moral behaviour</u> — doing what's <u>right</u> — is important. But, many Jews argue that you should do good things just because that's <u>what's right</u>, not to be <u>rewarded</u> in the World to Come or in Gan Eden.

Judaism teaches that many people can eventually enter Gan Eden

Different Jewish groups have different ideas about what happens in the afterlife — but they all believe in some sort of life after death. Try to remember the different ideas from this page.

Life After Death: Islam

Islam has very <u>definite teachings</u> when it comes to life after death.

The **Soul** is the **Real Person**

1) Muslims believe that the soul will be <u>judged</u> after death.

2) Muslims call life after death <u>akhirah</u> — it's one of the key Islamic beliefs.

3) Islam teaches that no events during our earthly lives are accidental — we are being <u>tested</u>, and the way we act in this life will <u>determine</u> what happens to us after we die.

4) A key teaching of Islam is that we remain in the <u>grave</u> after death in a state called the 'cold sleep' until the <u>Day of Judgement</u>. On this day, Allah will judge <u>everyone</u> — not just Muslims. This is why Muslims are <u>buried</u>, not cremated (see p.87).

The soul goes to **Jannah** (Paradise) or **Jahannam** (Hell)

1) Muslims believe that it's <u>too late</u> to beg forgiveness for any wrongdoing on <u>Judgement Day</u>.

2) Islam teaches that we are judged on:

> • our <u>character</u>   • our <u>reactions</u> to good and bad events in our lives   • our <u>way of life</u>

3) Muslims believe everything that happens is the <u>will of Allah</u> — so there's no point moaning about our circumstances. The important thing is that we react to them the <u>right</u> way.

4) The <u>reward</u> for those who have followed Allah well will be entry into <u>Jannah (Paradise)</u> — this is a place of <u>peace</u>, happiness and beauty.

5) Those who <u>don't believe</u> in Allah, or have committed <u>bad deeds</u>, are sent to <u>Jahannam</u> (or <u>Hell</u>) and are punished for eternity.

6) But Allah is also <u>merciful</u>, so many of those who have lived sinful lives may not be sent to Jahannam.

Being **Obedient** to **Allah** is vital for a Muslim

'<u>Islam</u>' literally means 'submission' or 'obedience' to Allah — <u>obedience</u> is the key to getting to <u>Paradise</u>. The reasoning is as follows:

1) Allah <u>expects</u> obedience, and obedience is a Muslim's <u>duty</u>.

2) If a Muslim does his or her duty, that person will <u>please</u> Allah.

3) If a person pleases Allah enough, they will be sent to <u>Paradise</u> after they die.

4) And if Allah is <u>not</u> pleased with someone, they will be <u>punished</u> after they die.

Allah will decide if we go to Jannah or Jahannam

So, there are some new terms to learn on this page, but the main idea is the same as for Christianity and Judaism — if you're obedient in this life, you will live on in Paradise.

Life After Death: Other Religions

Buddhism, Sikhism and Hinduism have <u>similar</u> ideas about life after death.

Buddhists, Sikhs and Hindus believe in Reincarnation

1) Buddhists, Sikhs and Hindus believe that we exist in a <u>cycle</u> of life, death and rebirth. When we die, our spirit <u>leaves</u> our body and finds a <u>new</u> one.

2) This spirit can begin a new life in a <u>human</u>, <u>animal</u> or <u>spiritual</u> form. The quality of the new life depends on the person's <u>actions</u> in their previous life — if they acted <u>morally</u>, the spirit might take a <u>human</u> form, but if they lived a sinful life, then the spirit could end up having an <u>animal</u> or <u>unhappy</u> form.

The law of Karma determines what each Life is like

1) Our actions in this life affect what happens to us in the next — good deeds earn <u>positive karma</u>, but bad deeds result in <u>bad karma</u>.

2) If you build up good karma during a lifetime, you will be born into a <u>better</u> situation in your next life. But, if you earn <u>bad</u> karma, you will end up <u>suffering</u> more in the next life.

3) The ultimate <u>aim</u> is not to gain a higher status and a better life, but to be <u>free</u> from the cycle completely — this means an end to suffering. For Sikhs and Hindus, the only way out of the cycle is to achieve total <u>union</u> with God. For Buddhists, the only way out is to reach <u>enlightenment</u> (see p.110).

> Hindus believe that every living being has dharma — a duty. If they fulfil their dharma, they'll earn good karma.

Buddhists believe there are 6 Realms of life

<u>Buddhists</u> believe that there are 6 realms that you can be reborn into:

- <u>heaven</u> — where gods live
- the <u>human</u> realm
- the realm of <u>Asura</u> (angry gods)
- the realm of <u>hungry ghosts</u>
- the <u>animal</u> realm
- <u>hell</u> — a place of torture

> Sikhs believe a soul can only be freed from the cycle (achieve mukti) when it lives in human form — because only humans know the difference between right and wrong.

1) None of these places are <u>permanent</u>. Even if you go to <u>hell</u>, you don't stay there forever — you just have to stay long enough to pay off your <u>bad karma</u>.

2) If a person earns enough good karma they can achieve <u>liberation</u> or <u>nirvana</u> and finally be free from the cycle.

Buddhists, Sikhs and Hindus want to escape suffering

So the idea is pretty simple really — you try to be good in this life (and avoid bad karma), otherwise it'll come back to haunt you in the next life. Nobody wants to be reborn as a worm...

Questions

So, that's the end of Section 5 — let's see how much you can remember about rites of passage. So get your thinking cap on and work through the questions on these pages.

Warm-up Questions

1) How are babies baptised by Christians?
2) Describe one Muslim ritual which marks the birth of a baby.
3) What are the tefillin? (Judaism)
4) Name a religion that believes in the laws of karma.

Practice Questions

These questions might take a little longer to complete, but they're good practice.

1) Write down two reasons why:
   a) Becoming a Bar/Bat Mitzvah is important for young Jews.
   b) An adult baptism is different to a confirmation.

2) Copy out and complete this passage, adding the correct words from the list below:

   **funeral   Christians   deceased   resurrected
   support   bereaved   Prayers**

   a) Christians hold _____ services to mark the death of a loved one. The service can be comforting to the _____ because they are encouraged to believe that they will one day be reunited with the _____ .

   b) It doesn't matter if _____ are cremated or buried — they believe that their spirit will use a new body when it is _____ on Judgement Day.

   c) _____ are said for the bereaved during the service. Afterwards, the priest or minister will usually offer them _____ to cope with their grief.

3) Describe what Muslims believe about Jannah (Paradise) and Jahannam (Hell) and how this might affect how they live.

4) Copy and complete the passage below using the correct choice of words.
   Buddhists, **(Sikhs / Muslims)** and Hindus all believe that when we die, our spirit moves to a new body and starts a new life. This is called **(reincarnation / karma)**. The quality of the new **(soul / life)** depends on how the person lived in the **(previous / next)** life. If they were a **(bad / good)** person, and acted morally, they will be **(punished / rewarded)** with a good new life. However, if they lived an immoral life, they could be **(cremated / reborn)** into a worse situation.

Section Five — Summary Questions

These questions are a bit trickier than the Practice Questions, but keep trying with them until you're confident that you know all there is to know about rites of passage.

1) Explain the importance of godparents in a Christian infant baptism.

2) What is a dedication? Why do some Christians choose to give their child a dedication rather than an infant baptism?

3) Describe why Brit Milah is important to Jews.

4) Explain why it's important for a Muslim baby to hear the call to prayer moments after their birth.

5) Describe what happens during an aqiqah (or aqeeqah), and why it's important to Muslims.

6) Do you think it is important to mark the birth of a baby? Why? / Why not?

7) What does a Bar/Bat Mitzvah ceremony involve?

8) Describe what happens during a Christian confirmation.

9) Do you think a person should automatically be part of the same religious group as their parents? Why? / Why not?

10) Explain why mourning is an important process.

11) "Funerals are more for the living than the dead."
Discuss this statement, including different points of view, as well as your own viewpoint. You should refer to a religion in your answer.

12) Describe why it is important for Muslims to be buried and not cremated.

13) State two things that Christians believe about Heaven.

14) Explain how different Jewish beliefs about the resurrection may cause Jews to feel differently about cremation.

15) What do Jews believe will happen in the World to Come?

16) Explain the difference between Gan Eden and Gehinnom in Judaism.

17) State two things that Buddhists believe about the cycle of life, death and rebirth.

18) Explain how the law of karma works.

19) Do you think there is a life after death? Why? / Why not?

20) "Religious people are more likely to try to live a moral life than non-religious people."
Discuss this statement, including different points of view, as well as your own viewpoint. You should refer to a religion in your answer.

People and Animals: Christianity

Religions usually say be nice to other people. But what about <u>animals</u>...?

*Christianity says **Animals** come **Below People***

1) According to the Bible, God made the world, humankind was made to <u>populate</u> it, and animals were created for the <u>use</u> of humankind.

2) Christianity teaches that we should treat animals with <u>kindness</u>, but that they can be used to benefit humankind (as long as their <u>suffering</u> is considered).

3) Some Christians believe that money should not be '<u>wasted</u>' on animals when <u>human beings</u> are suffering.

4) Unlike some other religions, there are no specific <u>food laws</u> to be followed in Christianity. So <u>vegetarianism</u> (not eating meat) and <u>veganism</u> (not eating or using any animal products) are a matter of personal choice.

> *"...Rule over the fish of the sea and the birds of the air and over every living creature that moves on the ground."* **Genesis 1:28 NIV**

> **The Bible tells us that Jesus ate fish, and as a Jew he would have eaten meat at certain festivals.**

Animal Rights are Important to many Christians

Different branches of Christianity have different views on <u>animal rights</u> issues:

- The <u>Anglican Church</u> teaches that we should consider how we use <u>animals</u> — to make sure they're not caused <u>unnecessary suffering</u>. This can be applied to <u>farming</u>, animal <u>experimentation</u> and <u>domestic</u> animals.

- The <u>Roman Catholic</u> Church tolerates things like <u>animal experimentation</u>, but only if it could bring about a potential <u>benefit</u> to humankind (e.g. if the experiments could lead to the development of life-saving medicines).

- Certain denominations are generally <u>opposed</u> to any ill-treatment of animals — especially for our <u>pleasure</u>. For example, the <u>Society of Friends</u> (<u>Quakers</u>) frown upon zoos, animal circuses, hunting and the wearing of fur.

Animals are important to Christians, but not as important as people

I bet you thought I was just going to say something like, 'Christians say be nice to furry things'. Well, they do — to an extent. But animal experimentation complicates things a bit.

People and Animals: Judaism and Islam

Judaism and Islam both have clear rules about how <u>animals</u> should be treated.

Judaism says that **Cruelty** to animals is **Forbidden**

1) The <u>Noahide Laws</u> (laws given to Adam, and later to Noah, after the Flood) contain a law which <u>forbids cruelty</u> to animals. Animals are here to <u>help</u> us, and not to be <u>abused</u>.

> **"The righteous care for the needs of their animals,"** Proverbs 12:10 NIV

2) In Judaism, if <u>meat</u> is to be eaten, the animal must be slaughtered in a <u>humane</u> manner. This involves cutting the throat of the animal with a very sharp blade to bring about a <u>quick death</u>.

3) <u>Experiments</u> on animals may be tolerated if they result in a benefit for humankind, but only as a <u>last resort</u>.

4) Cruel sports (e.g. <u>bullfighting</u>) are seen as an <u>abuse</u> of G-d's creatures. <u>Hunting</u> for sport is also frowned upon.

> **"...you shall not do any work, neither you... nor your ox, your donkey or any of your animals..."** Deuteronomy 5:14 NIV

5) The Torah says that animals deserve a day off on the <u>Sabbath</u>, just like people:

Muslims believe that **Allah** loves **All Animals**

1) Muslims believe that they have been appointed <u>khalifah</u> (trustees) of the Earth. This is the idea that we should <u>look after</u> the Earth in Allah's name. This includes taking care of <u>animals</u>.

2) Muslims also believe that animals exist to be used by <u>humans</u>, but they should still be treated <u>kindly</u>.

3) Cruelty to animals is <u>forbidden</u>, as is their use simply for our <u>pleasure</u>.

4) Making animals fight and hunting for <u>sport</u> are not allowed.

5) Animals that are going to be <u>eaten</u> must be killed according to <u>Sharia law</u> (see p.47) — this includes being treated <u>well</u> before they are killed and being <u>slaughtered humanely</u>.

> **"...when you slaughter, slaughter in a good way. So every one of you should sharpen his knife, and let the slaughtered animal die comfortably."** Prophet Muhammad (Sahih Muslim)

Jews believe animals deserve a day off on the Sabbath too

Jews and Muslims try to treat animals with kindness, even though they believe they exist to make life easier for humans. Muslims try to treat even those they're going to eat as well as possible.

Environmental Issues: Christianity

Unfortunately, our planet is suffering from many man-made problems.

Our **Small Planet** has some **Big Problems**

The environmental problems facing the world include:

- global warming (caused by the emission of greenhouse gases)
- deforestation
- extinction of animal and plant species
- pollution (leading to problems like acid rain)
- using up of irreplaceable natural resources

1) Developed countries are the worst (but not the only) offenders. Businesses often put profit before the welfare of the planet.

2) Some governments are more focused on short-term benefits than long-term care for the planet.

3) Richer countries sometimes criticise governments in developing nations when they harm the environment (e.g. deforestation). However, the developing nations will often justify themselves by saying that they're only doing now what more developed countries did in the past.

4) There are things we can do, as individuals, to help minimise our impact on the environment. For example, recycling helps conserve natural resources, and walking more, using public transport and using alternative energy resources (e.g. solar power) help to reduce greenhouse gas emissions.

Christians believe that **God** expects us to care for the **Earth**

1) Christians of all denominations believe that God created the Earth, and expects us to care for it — the idea of caring for the planet is called 'stewardship'.

2) Christianity upholds the belief that everything is interdependent (i.e. everything depends on everything else), so driving species of animal or plant to extinction, or harming the planet, eventually ends up harming us.

3) Christian organisations such as CAFOD, Christian Aid and Tearfund are concerned with putting this responsibility into practice. They put pressure on governments and industries to think more about how we are abusing the planet.

> "The earth is the Lord's, and everything in it, the world, and all who live in it; for he founded it upon the seas and established it upon the waters." Psalm 24:1-2 NIV

> "You made him [humankind] a little lower than the heavenly beings and crowned him with glory and honour. You made him ruler over the works of your hands; you put everything under his feet" Psalm 8:5-6 NIV

> "We have a responsibility to create a balanced policy between consumption and conservation." Pope John Paul II, 1988

Stewardship is the idea that it's our job to care for the planet

It's a massive responsibility, but I guess there are plenty of us to share the load. The idea of stewardship encourages Christians to take better care of the Earth — as it's a gift from God.

Environmental Issues: Judaism and Islam

Islam and Judaism have pretty similar ideas to Christianity when it comes to environmental issues. All three religions teach that God has put us in charge of the Earth.

Concern for the **Natural World** is important to **Judaism**

1) Jews also believe in the concept of stewardship (see p.96).

2) G-d's creations should remain as he intended, and we have no right to abuse them. Everything is interdependent, with trees being seen as particularly important.

3) Jews also believe that as custodians, they're responsible for making the world better — this is called tikkun olam ('perfecting the world').

4) Tikkun olam isn't just about the environment — it's a general ideal that includes helping the poor, and behaving morally.

5) Another Jewish moral principle is Bal Tashchit ('do not destroy or waste'). Although this principle is applied to life in general — you shouldn't waste fuel or deliberately ruin your possessions — many Jews consider it to be an important environmental principle.

> "The Lord God took the man and put him in the Garden of Eden to work it and take care of it."
> Genesis 2:15 NIV

Muslims will be **Judged** on how they **Treat** the **World**

1) Muslim teaching on environmental issues is very similar to that of Judaism — we are seen as trustees (khalifah).

2) Muslims believe that Allah created the whole world, so it must not be damaged.

3) At the Day of Judgement we'll have to answer for any ill-treatment of the planet and its resources.

4) The Earth is seen as being a product of the love of Allah, so we should treat it with love.

> "...[Adhere to] the fitrah (nature) of Allah upon which He has created [all] people. No change should there be in the creation of Allah..." Qur'an 30:30

> Dr Abdullah Omar Nasseef stated at the 1986 World Wide Fund for Nature conference that "His [Allah's] trustees are responsible for maintaining the unity of his creation, the integrity of the Earth, its flora and fauna, its wildlife and natural environment."

Allah put love into making the Earth, so we should love it in return

Muslims believe that we'll be judged on how well we've done in our roles as khalifah (trustees). Jews and Muslims, like Christians, think it's important to take care of our beautiful planet.

Caring for the Planet: Sikhism and Hinduism

Here are some <u>Sikh</u> and <u>Hindu</u> beliefs about how human beings should treat the <u>Earth</u>.

*Sikhs try to live in **Harmony** with the **Universe***

1) <u>Sikhs</u> believe that the world and everything within it was created by <u>Waheguru</u> (God).

"The sky, the earth, the trees, and the water — all are the Creation of the Lord."
Guru Granth Sahib p.723

2) The <u>Guru Granth Sahib</u> (see p.48) teaches that humans and animals are <u>both</u> important — so animals must be treated with <u>respect</u>.

3) Sikhs believe that every living thing has the opportunity to live a good life — to fulfil its <u>duties</u> in order to be <u>liberated</u> from the cycle of life, death and rebirth (see p.91).

4) <u>Hunting</u> for fun is not allowed in Sikhism, and <u>killing</u> animals for food that you don't really need is also frowned upon.

5) Sikhs believe that we're all closely linked to the environment, so taking care of the Earth is in our own <u>best interests</u>. So <u>polluting</u> and contributing to other environmental problems go against the gurus' main principles.

*Hindus believe in a **Respect** for **All Life***

1) Some Hindus see the Earth as a revelation of <u>Devi</u> (the female aspect of the divine), so it must be <u>respected</u>.

2) Hindus believe in <u>karma</u> and <u>reincarnation</u>, so if we <u>mistreat</u> the Earth or <u>abuse</u> its resources, we are causing future problems for <u>ourselves</u>.

3) However, some Hindus believe that it's up to us to <u>decide</u> how we use the Earth. This causes some <u>conflict</u> in India between those who want to <u>exploit</u> the environment for <u>development</u> and those who'd rather <u>protect</u> and <u>preserve</u> it.

4) Hinduism teaches that although animals are <u>inferior</u> to humans, they should be treated <u>well</u>. Hindus believe they could have been an animal in a <u>past</u> life, so they treat animals, to some extent, how they'd hope to be treated <u>themselves</u>.

5) Many Hindu <u>gods</u> have animal forms. For example, the god <u>Vishnu</u> had various <u>animal avatars</u> (see p.35) such as a <u>fish</u>, a <u>tortoise</u> and a <u>boar</u>.

6) Many Hindus are <u>vegetarian</u> because they believe in the concept of <u>ahimsa</u> (<u>non-violence</u>).

7) <u>Cows</u> in particular are considered sacred to Hindus because they are linked to the god Krishna — killing them is <u>banned</u>.

8) <u>Trees</u> are treated with particular <u>respect</u> — they are the most important type of plant life and are even thought to have <u>souls</u>.

Cows are sacred to Hindus

To Hindus, cows are definitely the most important animal, but all other living beings should be respected too. Trees are thought to be pretty special — more so than all the other plants.

Caring for the Planet: Buddhism and Other Beliefs

Not all environmental opinions are based on religion. This page is about what <u>Buddhists</u> believe and also what people might think about the environment regardless of religion.

*Buddhists believe that we're **All** part of '**Nature**'*

1) In Buddhism there is not a strong distinction between <u>humans</u> and <u>nature</u> — we are <u>part</u> of nature. Human beings are part of the cycle of life, death and rebirth along with every other living thing.

2) Buddhists believe in the laws of <u>karma</u> — they believe that environmental <u>problems</u> are the <u>result</u> of our actions.

3) Buddhists think that it is <u>wrong</u> and <u>unfair</u> to take resources that we don't need because there might not be enough for <u>future generations</u>.

4) <u>Vegetarianism</u> is not an essential part of Buddhism, but it's believed that killing animals and eating meat results in <u>bad karma</u>.

5) <u>Plants</u> are also respected, and <u>trees</u> in particular are often <u>protected</u> by Buddhists — some have even been ordained as Buddhist <u>monks</u> in order to protect them.

*Caring for the **Earth** is not only a **Religious Issue***

1) It's <u>not</u> just religious people who want to take care of the Earth. Many people want to <u>preserve</u> our planet for their <u>own</u> benefit and for the benefit of <u>future generations</u>.

2) Lots of people try to take better care of the environment by doing things such as <u>recycling</u> or <u>using public transport</u>.

3) On a <u>larger scale</u>, many countries are making an effort to lower the <u>impact</u> their nation has on the planet. For example, this could be by preventing <u>deforestation</u>, or by trying to develop energy sources that <u>don't</u> harm the environment.

4) Many of the world's resources are limited — they will run out one day. Using up <u>resources</u> now could lead to <u>shortages</u> in the future, which could lead to <u>tensions</u> between nations over resources.

Everyone agrees that our world is worth looking after

So, there you have it — Christians, Jews, Muslims, Sikhs, Hindus, Buddhists *and* non-religious people all try to take care of the environment. Try to remember some of the reasons why.

Questions

That's another section done and dusted — brilliant stuff. Try these questions to see how much you really understood.

Warm-up Questions

1) What is veganism?
2) Explain the views of one religion on animal rights.
3) Name three environmental problems that the world is facing today.
4) Name two Christian organisations that are concerned with protecting the environment.
5) Explain what Judaism teaches about caring for the environment.

Practice Questions

Now that you're into the swing of things, try these practice questions.

1) Copy out and complete these sentences, adding the correct words from the list below:

    Noahide   cruelty   abused   humankind   slaughtered

    benefit   meat   animals   Jews   appointed

    a) Christianity teaches that _____ should be cared for, but also that they were created by God to help _____. This means that many Christians accept animal testing if it might _____ humans.

    b) Jews believe that animals are on Earth to help us, but they shouldn't be _____. Adam, and later Noah, were given a set of laws called the _____ Laws which contained a law forbidding _____ to animals. _____ also believe that animals should have a day of rest on the Sabbath.

    c) Muslims believe that Allah has _____ them to take care of the Earth and everything on it. Eating _____ is allowed, but animals that are going to be eaten must be treated well beforehand, and should be _____ humanely.

2) Explain why members of the following religions try to treat the Earth with respect:
    a) Sikhism
    b) Hinduism
    c) Buddhism

Section Six — Summary Questions

You know the drill by now. Try these questions — for any you can't do, look back through the section to find the answer and then have another go. Keep trying until you can do them all.

1) What is the difference between vegetarianism and veganism?

2) Do you think humans are more valuable than animals? Why? / Why not?

3) Briefly explain why a Christian might eat meat.

4) Explain why some Christians accept animal testing.

5) Why might Jews disagree with sports like bullfighting?

6) Explain what Jews believe about experiments on animals.

7) Briefly explain the rules covering the eating of meat in Islam.

8) What is stewardship? (Christianity)

9) What is tikkun olam? (Judaism)

10) Explain how the principle of Bal Tashchit affects how Jews live their lives.

11) Explain the concept of khalifah. (Islam)

12) Explain why Sikhs believe that they should take care of the planet.

13) Explain why some religions teach that taking care of the planet is the same as taking care of ourselves.

14) Name two living things that Hindus particularly respect.

15) Why might many Buddhists choose to be vegetarians?

16) Give two ways in which you could reduce your impact on the environment.

17) Do you think being religious might make a person care more about preserving the environment for future generations? Why? / Why not?

18) "It doesn't matter how we treat animals."
    Discuss this statement, including different points of view, as well as your own viewpoint.
    You should refer to a religion in your answer.

19) "The world is not ours to destroy."
    Discuss this statement, including different points of view, as well as your own viewpoint.
    You should refer to a religion in your answer.

20) "Environmental problems are our own fault."
    Discuss this statement, including different points of view, as well as your own viewpoint.
    You should refer to a religion in your answer.

Causes of Suffering

Loads of <u>bad things</u> happen in the world. These issues often cause people to ask "<u>Why?</u>".
For many religious people, the bigger question is: "Why is <u>God</u> letting this happen?"

*Suffering can be either **Human**-made or **Natural***

Suffering can be divided into <u>two types</u>:

Suffering caused by humans

1) This is when suffering is brought about by the <u>cruel</u> or <u>careless</u> actions of <u>people</u>.

2) This includes things like <u>murder</u>, <u>war</u>, <u>rape</u> and <u>torture</u>.

3) The person causing the suffering is often able to make a <u>choice</u> about what is morally <u>right or wrong</u>.

Suffering caused by nature

1) This kind of suffering is <u>caused by the world</u> in which we live, and is <u>no one's 'fault'</u>.

2) This includes things like <u>disease</u>, <u>floods</u>, <u>earthquakes</u> and <u>hurricanes</u>.

3) However, many <u>recent natural disasters</u> may have been partly caused by <u>human interference</u> in the natural world, raising the question of whether that makes those events <u>human-made</u>.

*Suffering can lead people to **Question** their **Faith***

1) <u>Suffering</u> leads some people to <u>question</u> their belief in God — or even to <u>reject</u> their faith.

2) This might be because they can't believe that a god who is <u>good</u> would <u>allow</u> such things to happen, or because they feel that their <u>prayers</u> are <u>not being answered</u> (i.e. they think God <u>could</u> help, but <u>doesn't</u>).

Unanswered prayers

Christianity, Judaism and Islam teach that <u>no sincere prayer</u> goes unheard or unanswered. And that if a prayer seems to be unanswered, it's just that we can't <u>understand</u> God's reply. Since no human being can ever know <u>God's plan</u>, it's impossible to say what's really best for us.

3) Other people argue that God can't be very <u>powerful</u> if he is <u>unable</u> to prevent suffering (i.e. God <u>can't</u> help, even if he wanted to).

4) Since Christianity, Judaism and Islam all teach that God is both <u>good</u> and <u>all-powerful</u>, suffering presents them with a <u>challenge</u>, which they meet in various ways (see p.103-108).

Suffering can be caused by the actions of humans

This isn't the most cheerful page in the book, but it's still worth having a good read of it.
Many religions focus a lot of their prayers and efforts on helping people who are suffering.

Suffering: Christianity

There are many examples of suffering in the <u>Bible</u> — they help to explain <u>why</u> suffering exists.

Suffering Entered the world after The Fall

1) <u>Christianity</u> teaches that evil and suffering <u>entered</u> the world as a result of <u>Adam and Eve</u> (the first human beings) <u>disobeying</u> God in the Garden of Eden. This switch from a perfect world to one containing suffering is known as 'the Fall'.

2) Because of the Fall, every human being is said to have a <u>sinful nature</u>, and therefore is inclined to do the <u>wrong</u> thing. This is the idea of <u>original sin</u>.

3) <u>Suffering</u> is often seen as a <u>test of faith</u> — <u>God</u> has his <u>reasons</u> for it (even if we <u>don't know</u> what they are). Christians believe that they should try to <u>help</u> people who are suffering — both <u>practically</u> and by <u>praying</u>.

4) Many Christians believe that it's when we <u>suffer</u> that we are closest to <u>Jesus</u>, who suffered and died for all humankind.

Job Trusted God and so Accepted suffering

The story of <u>Job</u>, in the <u>Old Testament</u>, is used by Christians to help them accept <u>suffering</u>:

Job's Trials (The Book of Job)

• Job was a <u>good</u> man and a <u>loyal</u> servant of God. One day, God used him as an example to Satan, saying that Job always <u>obeyed</u> and <u>trusted</u> him.

• However, Satan said that Job was a bad example, because God had <u>blessed</u> him with a <u>family</u> and <u>wealth</u>. Satan suggested that Job only loved God because he was <u>happy</u>, and that he wouldn't be so loyal and trusting if he was made to <u>suffer</u>.

• So, God allowed Satan to make Job <u>suffer</u> to see if he would change his attitude.

• Job lost his property, his cattle, and his sons and daughters, but he didn't <u>curse</u> God — he said, "The Lord gave and the Lord has taken away; may the name of the Lord be praised" (Job 1:21 NIV).

• Job was made to suffer even more, this time with physical <u>pain</u>. He began to question why God let this happen to a faithful person like him. He couldn't understand why he was being <u>punished</u>.

• In the end, Job came to the conclusion that God is all-powerful and knows what he is doing — and that suffering must be <u>accepted</u> because we can't really understand the world or <u>God's plan</u>.

God tested Job by making him suffer

Christians believe that suffering exists for a reason — it's all part of God's plan. Many think suffering is God's way of testing how much they trust him and how strong their faith is.

Suffering: Christianity

Christians believe that God sent Jesus partly to reduce the suffering on Earth — many of them try to follow Jesus's example by helping people who are suffering.

Christians believe that Jesus Suffered on their behalf

1) Christians believe that God lived on Earth in the form of Jesus, as God's answer to the problem of human suffering.

2) Jesus performed miracles which helped to relieve people's suffering.

> "Jesus healed many who had various diseases. He also drove out many demons" Mark 1:34 NIV

3) Christians believe that Jesus died on our behalf to save us from our sins. As a consequence, we can enter Heaven after death, where there is no more suffering.

Christians have a Duty to Relieve Poverty

1) One of the biggest causes of suffering is poverty.

2) All Christian denominations want wealth to be shared more fairly. A key question is whether wealth ultimately belongs to God, and should therefore be used for the good of everyone.

3) Jesus spoke of the necessity of giving up all wealth and possessions to follow him. However, no Christian denomination teaches that having wealth is wrong as such.

4) Some churches are rich — this worries some believers, especially because of Jesus's teachings.

5) A number of Christian organisations try to tackle poverty — one example is Christian Aid:

Case Study — Christian Aid

Christian Aid works globally to relieve poverty. It raises money through donations, events and collections. Most of Christian Aid's work is in development in poorer countries abroad. Although it contributes to emergency disaster relief, it believes the best way to help people is by helping them to help themselves. It sets up projects in the developing world, drawing on local people's skills.

Christians believe all wealth ultimately belongs to God

Charity is an important issue for Christians — there's a lot of suffering in the world and they feel that it's their responsibility to do what they can to help those in need.

Suffering: Judaism

Jews have a similar attitude towards suffering as Christians — these pages explain the details.

Jews believe that G-d created both **Good** and **Evil**

1) Modern Judaism has no concept of a devil fighting against G-d and tempting people into doing evil deeds. It is believed that G-d created everything — and that includes both good and evil.

2) The Book of Job in the Hebrew Bible contains an important lesson about suffering. It suggests that we should accept it as part of G-d's plan (see p.103).

3) Judaism teaches that we have free will and are able to choose what we do, but that we are prone to making mistakes.

Jews believe that **Good** can come out of **Suffering**

1) Like many Christians, Jews may also respond to suffering and evil through prayer.

2) The Jewish approach often stresses the idea that good can come out of suffering. Suffering can bring people closer to each other and closer to G-d.

3) Jews don't try to explain the presence of suffering. They believe that it's better to help those who are suffering than to question why they are suffering.

4) Suffering allows people to make sacrifices for others and draw on their inner strength.

5) Suffering is a part of the human experience and must be accepted.

6) An example of human response to suffering is the work carried out by JCORE (The Jewish Council for Racial Equality):

JCORE

JCORE is a Jewish organisation, based in the UK. They campaign for the rights of asylum seekers, raise awareness of the problems that immigrants face and offer all sorts of practical help. For example, they have a Refugee Doctors Mentoring Project that gives information and practical help to trained immigrant doctors, helping them to retrain and practise in the UK.

Suffering gives us the chance to help others

Jews don't focus on why suffering exists. Instead, they try to help those who are suffering, which in turn helps make them better people. The main ideas are the same as in Christianity.

Suffering: Judaism

This page is about one of the <u>worst</u> examples of mass <u>suffering</u> in Jewish history, and how Jews have managed to <u>cope</u> with it.

The **Holocaust** — *the Nazis'* **Extermination** *of* **Jews**

1) For <u>many centuries</u>, Jews living in Europe faced a lot of <u>persecution</u>.

2) Hatred of Jews is known as <u>anti-Semitism</u>, and it spread through many countries. The fact that many Jews regarded themselves as <u>loyal citizens</u> of these countries didn't stop this from happening.

3) During the 1920s, <u>Germany</u> faced huge economic problems. The National Socialist (<u>Nazi</u>) Party blamed '<u>non-Aryan</u>' people (i.e. those who weren't originally from Northern Europe) living in Germany — especially the <u>Jews</u>.

4) On coming to power in 1933, its leader, <u>Adolf Hitler</u>, gradually deprived the Jews of their <u>rights</u>.

5) Eventually Hitler introduced the <u>Final Solution</u> — the plan to wipe out the Jews completely. During World War Two (1939-1945), the Nazis built <u>concentration camps</u> and <u>extermination camps</u> where huge numbers of Jews perished in <u>gas chambers</u>.

The Holocaust caused Jews to ask *"Where Was G-d?"*

The Holocaust caused serious <u>spiritual problems</u> for Jews — they considered questions like:

- If G-d exists, and is <u>good</u> and <u>all-powerful</u>, <u>how</u> could he allow this to happen to his <u>chosen people</u>?

Jews have come up with many <u>responses</u> to this type of question:

1) Some Jews have concluded that there is <u>no G-d</u>.

2) Some have concluded that if G-d exists, he either <u>doesn't care</u>, or is <u>powerless</u> to help.

3) Some Jews say that the Holocaust, and all suffering, is a <u>test of faith</u> — if good people always got the best things in life, everyone would be good for the wrong reasons.

4) Some Jews say that G-d could intervene to stamp out evil if he chose to. However, he gave all human beings <u>free will</u> and refuses to override this, even when it is abused. Also, it would be impossible for G-d to destroy all evil people, because <u>no one</u> is completely evil or completely good.

5) Some Jews regard all those who died in the Holocaust as <u>martyrs</u> for the faith, and see their martyrdom as 'sanctifying the name of G-d'.

6) Some say the most important thing is to <u>keep practising</u> Judaism, or Hitler will have won.

Jews have faced a lot of suffering throughout history

Nobody knows why there's so much suffering in the world, but Jews try to focus on doing something good to prevent or ease it. So, maybe good can sometimes come from suffering...

Suffering: Islam

Muslims believe that suffering is closely linked to <u>sinful</u> actions and that Allah will be <u>testing</u> how they cope with suffering.

Islam *says we have the* Choice...

1) Islam teaches that <u>humankind</u> was created with <u>free will</u> — people can <u>choose</u> to follow Allah, or <u>choose</u> to do wrong (which can lead to suffering).

2) Allah allows Shaytan (the devil) to <u>tempt</u> humankind away from the right path. We have <u>free will</u> so can choose whether to give in to temptation or not — it's a test of <u>faith</u>.

3) Muslims believe that by focusing on <u>Allah's message</u> in the Qur'an, they can <u>protect</u> themselves from <u>Shaytan's</u> schemes.

4) Islam teaches that if we choose to act against the will of Allah we will have to answer for that wrongdoing on the <u>Day of Judgement</u>.

5) <u>Everything</u> that happens is part of Allah's plan. Allah has <u>good reasons</u> for allowing evil, including evil caused by nature (see p.102), to occur — even if that isn't immediately apparent to us.

6) Evil also gives people the chance to <u>do good</u>:

   - It gives us the opportunity to <u>help</u> those in need.
   - It demonstrates that we can act with <u>patience</u> and <u>faith</u>.

The Qur'an *says "We Will Surely Test You"*

The following passage is taken from the <u>Qur'an 2:155-156</u>:

> "And We will surely test you with something of fear and hunger and a loss of wealth and lives and fruits, but give good tidings to the patient, who, when disaster strikes them, say, 'Indeed we belong to Allah, and indeed to Him we will return.' "

This is remarkably similar to the message of the Book of Job (see p.103).

1) The idea here is that <u>suffering should be accepted</u>. Muslims believe that, despite suffering in <u>this life</u>, there will be <u>joy in the next</u> as Allah is <u>compassionate</u>.

2) Muslims believe that Allah is <u>testing</u> them when he makes them suffer — if they stay <u>faithful</u> to him in times of suffering then they will be <u>rewarded</u> in the next life.

Muslims try to accept suffering

You'll notice similarities between Muslim, Christian and Jewish beliefs about suffering. Muslims believe that Allah lets the devil tempt us to see if we'll give in to temptation or not.

Suffering: Islam

Like followers of most other religions, Muslims believe that they have a <u>duty</u> to help those who are suffering.

Muslims try to Help those who are Suffering

1) Muslims believe that those who are suffering should be treated with <u>kindness</u>.

2) The Qur'an mentions the importance of <u>charity</u> — if you help others you will be <u>rewarded</u> on Judgement Day:

> **"Those who spend their wealth [in Allah's way] by night and by day, secretly and publicly — they will have their reward with their Lord. And no fear will there be concerning them, nor will they grieve." Qur'an 2:274**

'In Allah's way' means '<u>charitably</u>' here.

3) <u>Helping</u> those in need is a way of <u>thanking Allah</u> for all he has given you.

4) Muslim <u>charities</u>, including <u>Islamic Aid</u> and <u>Islamic Relief UK</u>, work to help reduce the suffering around the world.

Islamic Aid

Islamic Aid is an international Muslim organisation dedicated to reducing <u>poverty</u>. Their work in the UK centres on <u>improving links</u> between Muslims based in the UK and communities elsewhere, to raise awareness of the <u>injustice</u> and <u>poverty</u> in developing countries.

Islamic Relief UK

Islamic Relief UK was established in <u>1984</u>. The group is inspired by their <u>faith</u> to try to help as many people as possible, no matter where they come from or what <u>religion</u> they follow.

The charity began by giving <u>aid</u> to those affected by <u>wars</u> or <u>natural disasters</u>, but now they have offices all around the world, and also aim to reduce <u>long-term</u> poverty and suffering.

Helping others can lead to rewards in the next life

Muslims believe that helping others during this lifetime can lead to rewards on the Day of Judgement. See how many points you can remember from these two pages without looking.

Suffering: Buddhism

Suffering is a key part of Buddhism — this page will explain <u>what</u> Buddhists believe suffering is and <u>where</u> it comes from.

Buddhists accept the *Four Noble Truths*

The <u>essence</u> of the Buddha's teachings — suffering and how to end it — can be found in the <u>Four Noble Truths</u>:

1) The truth of <u>suffering</u> (dukkha)
2) The truth of the <u>cause</u> of suffering (samudaya)
3) The truth of <u>freedom</u> from suffering (nirodha)
4) The truth of the <u>path to freedom</u> from suffering (magga)

The first Noble Truth — *Dukkha*

Buddhists recognise different types of suffering (dukkha).

1) The <u>physical</u> and <u>mental</u> suffering that comes with <u>birth</u>, <u>old age</u>, <u>illness</u> and <u>death</u>.
2) The <u>disappointment</u> we feel when life doesn't live up to our <u>expectations</u>.
3) Also, even <u>pleasure</u> ends in a suffering of sorts, because <u>satisfaction</u> is only <u>temporary</u>. When you get what you want, you <u>stop</u> appreciating it and are no longer <u>fulfilled</u>.

The Buddha said suffering is caused by *Desire*

1) In the second Noble Truth, the Buddha explained <u>why</u> there is suffering in the world.
2) Sometimes suffering might seem to have an <u>obvious explanation</u> — for example, a cut knee might be caused by slipping on some ice. But, according to Buddha's teachings, <u>misplaced desire</u> (<u>Tanha</u>) is the root of all evil and the cause of all suffering.
3) As human beings, no matter how successful we are, we <u>never stay satisfied</u> for long.
4) Desire is believed to come in three forms — they are <u>the three roots of evil</u>:

- Desire for <u>items</u> and <u>pleasant feelings</u>.
- Desire to continue to <u>live</u> and <u>exist</u>.
- Desire to <u>avoid unpleasant experiences</u>.

Suffering is the first noble truth

Buddhism teaches that suffering is unavoidable in this world — all human beings suffer. Even the most lucky and successful people suffer because feeling satisfied is only temporary.

Suffering: Buddhism

This page is more <u>positive</u> — the Buddha had clear advice on how we should act to be freed from suffering.

The third **Noble Truth** says **Freedom** from suffering is **Possible**

1) Buddhists believe that to be rid of <u>suffering</u>, you must stop <u>wanting too much</u>.

2) The Buddha freed himself from suffering by controlling his <u>emotions</u> and <u>desires</u>.

3) This freedom is part of <u>enlightenment</u>, and is referred to as achieving <u>nirvana</u>. It is believed to be a <u>state of mind</u> that all humans can reach.

4) Someone who has become enlightened is filled with <u>compassion</u> for all living things and has no <u>negative</u> emotions or <u>fears</u>.

5) After <u>death</u>, the enlightened person is freed from the <u>cycle</u> of life, death and rebirth (see p.91), so their suffering ends <u>forever</u>.

The **Eightfold Path** explains how to reach **Enlightenment**

The <u>Eightfold Path</u> is the Buddha's advice for reaching enlightenment — it's the <u>fourth Noble Truth</u>. Buddhists try to follow the eight points during their life to be <u>released from suffering</u>:

1) <u>Right understanding</u> — learning and accepting the Buddha's teaching.

2) <u>Right intention</u> — having good will and wanting to do what's right.

3) <u>Right speech</u> — speaking the truth and avoiding abusive language or gossip.

4) <u>Right action</u> — acting peacefully and kindly, and avoiding overindulgence.

5) <u>Right livelihood</u> — making a living in a way that doesn't cause harm.

6) <u>Right effort</u> — trying to keep a positive state of mind.

7) <u>Right mindfulness</u> — building awareness of the body, sensations, and states of mind.

8) <u>Right concentration</u> — developing the mental focus necessary to seek enlightenment.

Buddhism teaches that desire is the root of all evil

Remember, Buddhists acknowledge that not all desire is evil — the desires to help others or to have a greater understanding of Buddhism are definitely good things which reduce suffering.

Questions

Suffering isn't the most cheerful of topics, but responding to it is a key part of many religions. Many religious believers think it's how we respond to that suffering that shows what kind of person we are. It would be easy to be a good person if the world was perfect...

Warm-up Questions

1) Describe what is meant by 'suffering caused by humans'.
2) Explain how Christianity explains the existence of suffering.
3) Briefly describe the story of Job.
4) Explain how good can come from suffering.
5) According to the Buddha, what is the main cause of suffering?

Practice Questions

Now you've got into the swing of things, try these practice questions.

1) Copy and complete the passage below using the correct choice of words.

Christianity, Judaism and Islam all teach that **(happiness / suffering)** is part of God's plan and it is a way for God to **(test / control)** how we will react in difficult situations and to see if we will remain faithful.

Many religious people believe that they have a duty to **(watch / help)** people who are suffering, which is why a number of **(charities / schools)** have religious backgrounds.

2) Briefly describe the work done by the organisations below:

a) Christian Aid

b) JCORE

c) Islamic Aid

3) Copy and complete the explanation of Buddhism's Four Noble Truths below.

1. The truth of _____ (dukkha)

2. The truth of the _____ (samudaya)

3. The truth of _____ (nirodha)

4. The truth of the _____ to freedom from suffering (magga)

4) Describe the different types of suffering according to Buddhism.

Section Seven — Summary Questions

Now give these Summary Questions a go — if you can answer all of them without looking back in the book, it'll prove that you've learnt the key points about religious views on suffering.

1) Give one example of suffering caused by humans and one example of suffering caused by nature.

2) Explain the importance of 'the Fall' in relation to suffering.

3) State two things that Christians believe about suffering.

4) Explain Christian attitudes towards wealth and poverty.

5) State two things that Jews believe about suffering.

6) Explain what Jews believe about free will.

7) Explain how Jews believe that good can come out of suffering.

8) Give an example of a question that the Holocaust caused some Jews to consider.

9) Explain what Muslims believe about Shaytan.

10) State two things that Muslims believe about suffering.

11) Explain why charity is important to Muslims.

12) "God/G-d/Allah cannot prevent suffering."

   Discuss this statement, including different points of view, as well as your own viewpoint. You should refer to a religion in your answer.

13) "Suffering should be accepted as the will of God/G-d/Allah."

   Discuss this statement, including different points of view, as well as your own viewpoint. You should refer to a religion in your answer.

14) Describe the work of one religious charity. Explain how its aims are linked to religion.

15) "It's hard to believe in God when the world is full of suffering."

   Discuss this statement, including different points of view, as well as your own viewpoint. You should refer to a religion in your answer.

16) Explain how even pleasure can be part of suffering, according to Buddhists.

17) State three things we desire which Buddhists believe cause us problems.

18) Explain how Buddhists think suffering can be overcome.

19) What is the purpose of the Eightfold Path?

20) "Suffering is caused by greed."

   Discuss this statement, including different points of view, as well as your own viewpoint. You should refer to a religion in your answer.

Holy Places

Judaism, Christianity and Islam all see some places as particularly <u>holy</u>.

Places connected to *Jesus* are *Holy* to *Christians*

1) Jesus lived in <u>Israel</u>, so there are many <u>holy places</u> there:

- Jesus was born in the town of <u>Bethlehem</u> and grew up in the village of <u>Nazareth</u>.
- Jesus taught all around <u>Galilee</u> — he is said to have performed several miracles there.
- He spent his last days in the city of <u>Jerusalem</u>.

2) <u>Rome</u> is viewed as a holy place by many Christians — Jesus's followers, <u>Peter</u> and <u>Paul</u>, were said to have been killed there for their beliefs.

3) Christian pilgrims visit holy places all over the world which are connected to saints or miracles, e.g. <u>Santiago de Compostela</u> in Spain and <u>Canterbury</u> in England.

Jerusalem is the most *Holy* place to *Jews*

1) <u>Jerusalem</u> was the home of the holy <u>Jewish Temple</u>.

2) The Temple was built by <u>King Solomon</u>. It was destroyed in 587 BCE, but later rebuilt, and was then destroyed again in 70 CE.

3) The only part of this Temple still left standing is the <u>Western Wall</u> — Jews still go there to <u>pray</u> and <u>mourn</u> for the Temple.

4) Many Jews visit places from Jewish history such as the <u>Shrine of the Book</u>, the Holocaust Memorial (<u>Yad Vashem</u>) or <u>the fortress of Masada</u>, where the Jews made their last stand against the Romans in 73 CE.

Every Muslim aims to go to *Makkah* at least once

1) <u>Makkah</u>, in <u>Saudi Arabia</u>, is the birthplace of <u>Muhammad</u>. It's also where <u>Allah</u> first spoke to Muhammad, so it's an important place for Muslims.

2) The <u>pilgrimage</u> to Makkah is called the <u>Hajj</u>. All Muslims have a religious <u>duty</u> to make the Hajj once in their lives, unless they are too <u>ill</u> or <u>poor</u>.

3) The city of <u>Madinah</u> is also holy to Muslims. This is because Muhammad and his followers <u>fled</u> to Madinah when they were persecuted in Makkah.

4) Muslims believe that one night <u>Muhammad</u> made a <u>miraculous</u> journey to <u>Jerusalem</u>, and from there to <u>Heaven</u> (see p.119). Because of this, Jerusalem is also a holy place for Muslims, particularly the <u>Al-Aqsa Mosque</u> and the <u>Dome of the Rock</u>.

Being in a holy place can make people feel close to God

Learn a few of the most important holy places on this page, and think about why they're important to believers. Then you can learn about some other holy places on the next page.

Holy Places

Most <u>Hindu</u>, <u>Sikh</u> and <u>Buddhist</u> holy places are in <u>India</u>.

*Many **Hindu Holy Places** are connected to **Gods** or **Saints***

1) Hindus believe that the <u>river Ganges</u> is sacred — they think of it as a <u>goddess</u> called <u>Ganga</u>.

2) <u>Pilgrims</u> flock to the Ganges every year — they believe <u>bathing</u> in the water there <u>washes away their sins</u>.

3) There are <u>seven</u> ancient <u>towns</u> which Hindus believe are especially holy. The most famous one is <u>Ayodhya</u>, where the god <u>Rama</u> is said to have been born.

*The **Golden Temple** is the key **Holy** place for **Sikhs***

1) Sikhism doesn't place much value on <u>pilgrimages</u>. This is an example of Guru Nanak dismissing the aspects of Hinduism which he believed were <u>meaningless</u> (see p.21).

2) However, Sikhs do value visits to famous <u>gurdwaras</u>, and places where gurus once lived, if the journeys are taken with <u>devotion</u>.

3) The <u>Golden Temple</u> (the Harmandir Sahib) is built on an island in a lake in <u>Amritsar</u>, a holy Sikh city. The original version of the Sikh holy book, the <u>Guru Granth Sahib</u>, is kept there during the day.

4) The <u>Five Thrones</u> (or <u>Five Takhts</u>) are five gurdwaras (see p.74-75) where <u>decisions</u> about Sikh <u>teachings</u> are made — these are also considered to be holy locations.

5) The village of <u>Talwandi</u>, in modern-day Pakistan, is also important to Sikhs because <u>Guru Nanak</u> (the first guru) was born there.

***Buddhism** has **Several** holy places connected to the **Buddha's** life*

1) The four most holy places in <u>Buddhism</u> are:

- <u>Lumbini</u> — where the Buddha was <u>born</u>
- <u>Bodh Gaya</u> — where the Buddha achieved <u>enlightenment</u> (see p.19)
- <u>Sarnath</u> — where the Buddha preached his first <u>sermon</u>
- <u>Kusinara</u> — where the Buddha <u>died</u>

> **Lumbini is in Nepal. The other places are in India.**

2) Other holy places are where the Buddha performed <u>miracles</u>.

3) There are many other Buddhist places of pilgrimage in <u>India</u>, <u>Nepal</u>, <u>Tibet</u>, <u>China</u> and elsewhere.

4) There used to be two famous statues of the Buddha at <u>Bamiyan</u> in Afghanistan, but they were <u>destroyed</u> in <u>2001</u>.

Every religion has holy places

Even though believers usually accept that God is everywhere, they all have certain places which they consider to be special or holy. Many holy places are linked to a religious person or event.

History of Jerusalem

People have believed that the city of <u>Jerusalem</u> in Israel is a <u>holy</u> place for centuries.

The **Hebrews** were **Promised** the land of **Canaan**

1) The Old Testament of the Bible says God <u>promised Abraham</u> that his descendants (known as <u>Hebrews</u>, <u>Israelites</u> or <u>Jews</u>) would have the land of <u>Canaan</u> to live in. This was called the <u>Promised Land</u>. It is roughly the modern state of <u>Israel</u>.

2) After being freed from slavery in Egypt (see p.14), the <u>Israelites</u> eventually took over the Promised Land.

3) <u>King David</u> was a great leader who made all the Jewish tribes into one <u>united Jewish kingdom</u> called <u>Israel</u>.

4) In about 1000 BCE, David captured <u>Jerusalem</u> and made it the <u>capital</u> of Israel.

5) At that time, there were several <u>sanctuaries</u> (holy places) in Israel, but the most important one was <u>Jerusalem</u>.

6) David's son, <u>King Solomon</u>, built a magnificent temple in Jerusalem to replace the old sanctuary — this was the <u>First Temple</u>.

Jerusalem was **Captured** by the **Babylonians**

1) The <u>Babylonians</u> (members of the ancient community of Babylon) captured Jerusalem and <u>destroyed</u> the First Temple in 586 BCE. Many Jews were taken to Babylon (in present-day Iraq) as slaves.

2) In 538 BCE the Jews were allowed to <u>return</u> to Jerusalem, and they slowly <u>rebuilt</u> the city and the Temple. The new structure is often called the <u>Second Temple</u>.

Then **Jerusalem** was ruled by **Greek Laws**

1) <u>Alexander the Great</u> was a <u>Greek</u> king who reigned over many nations.

2) Around 330 BCE, his empire was expanding, and Jerusalem was forced to follow <u>Greek</u> laws and customs.

3) Many years later, conflict began when an altar to the Greek gods was placed in the <u>Temple</u> — many Jews <u>left</u> Israel at this time.

4) This <u>struggle</u> lasted for <u>three years</u>, but the Temple was eventually restored to <u>Judaism</u>.

Israel was then part of the **Roman Empire**

1) Israel belonged to the Romans from 63 BCE, but a <u>Jewish king</u> was allowed to rule under them at Jerusalem. The Jews could still <u>worship</u> at the Temple — but they weren't <u>happy</u>.

2) Both the <u>Romans</u> and the <u>Jewish</u> religious authorities thought that Jesus was a <u>threat</u> — he said that he was the <u>Son of God</u>. So when he came to Jerusalem, they arrested him and had him <u>crucified</u>.

3) In 66 CE, the Jews <u>rebelled</u> against the Roman Empire, but they <u>lost</u>, and the Romans <u>recaptured</u> Jerusalem and destroyed the Second Temple in 70 CE.

History of Jerusalem

The history of Jerusalem continued to be <u>violent</u> as different groups fought over it.

Muslims built a Mosque on the Temple site in Jerusalem

1) During a period of Muslim rule, in 705 CE, the construction of the <u>Al-Aqsa Mosque</u> was completed. It was built on Temple Mount — the site of the ancient Jewish Temple.

2) Jerusalem is important to <u>Muslims</u> — they believe it was from here that <u>Muhammad</u> visited Heaven on the <u>Night Journey</u> (see p.119).

3) The most famous building near the mosque is the <u>Dome of the Rock</u>. It enshrines the rock from which believers say Muhammad <u>ascended to Heaven</u>.

Christian Crusaders Recaptured Jerusalem

1) In <u>1096</u> the <u>Pope</u> launched a <u>Crusade</u> — a war to make the holy land of Jerusalem Christian.

2) The <u>Crusaders</u> captured <u>Jerusalem</u> in 1099.

3) The Al-Aqsa Mosque was <u>converted</u> into a <u>church</u> and a <u>royal palace</u>.

4) It was changed back into a <u>mosque</u> when <u>Saladin</u> recaptured Jerusalem for the <u>Muslims</u> in 1187.

5) There were other <u>Crusades</u> after, but none of them <u>succeeded</u>.

Jerusalem was Split into two in 1948

1) After World War Two, many Jews were <u>exiled</u> from their home countries.

2) The modern state of <u>Israel</u> was founded as a home for these Jews. However, this meant that many of the <u>Palestinians</u> already living there were <u>forced to move</u>.

3) This led to a <u>civil war</u> between the <u>Jewish</u> and <u>Palestinian</u> <u>communities</u> in Israel in 1947-1948.

4) After the war, Jerusalem was <u>divided</u> into a Jewish area in the <u>west</u> of the city and a Palestinian area in the <u>east</u>.

5) The <u>Western Wall</u> was in the Palestinian part of the city. This meant that Jews could not pray there.

Jerusalem was Reunited

1) In 1967 there was <u>another</u> war between Israel and the Palestinians, known as the <u>Six-Day War</u>.

2) The Israelis recaptured the <u>Old City</u>, including the <u>Western Wall</u>. Jews and Muslims can both worship there now, although there is often trouble between them.

The history of Jerusalem is full of conflict

Jerusalem is considered to be a very sacred place — it's part of the Jewish Promised Land. But a lot of violence has taken place there over the years, as it's been occupied by different groups.

The Importance of Jerusalem: Christianity

Christians believe that Jesus was crucified in Jerusalem, so it's a holy place for them.

Jesus spent his Last Days on Earth in Jerusalem

1) Jesus and his followers made the pilgrimage to Jerusalem to celebrate the Passover festival (see p.61). Jesus was welcomed by the crowds, who called him the son of King David (see p.115).

2) During their final meal together, Jesus told his followers that the bread was his body and the wine was his blood. This meal is called the Last Supper.

3) Later, Jesus went to pray in the Garden of Gethsemane, where he was arrested. The authorities felt threatened by Jesus — he was popular, and if he claimed to be the heir of David they could be in trouble.

4) Jesus was sentenced to crucifixion at a place called Golgotha. He was forced to carry his cross before he was nailed to it.

5) He was placed in a tomb nearby — but afterwards, he was resurrected (raised back to life by God) and his tomb was found empty (see p.137).

6) Over the following days, many of Jesus's disciples said they had met him alive in various places around Jerusalem.

> Golgotha is also known as Calvary.

Many Christian Pilgrims go to Jerusalem

1) The Church of the Holy Sepulchre in Jerusalem is one of the most important places of pilgrimage for Christians. It's built on the place where Jesus is believed to have been was crucified. The tomb where Jesus was laid to rest is also nearby.

2) Many pilgrims also go to the Via Dolorosa (Latin for "Way of Sorrow") because it's the route Jesus took when he was forced to carry his cross to the place of crucifixion.

3) Pilgrims follow the route, stopping to pray at certain places, just as Jesus stopped when he was carrying the cross. These stopping places are called the Stations of the Cross.

4) Many pilgrims also visit Ein Karem, situated in southwest Jerusalem, because it's believed that John the Baptist was born there.

Jesus died and was resurrected in Jerusalem

Jerusalem is an important holy place for Christians. They visit the site where they believe Jesus died to save humankind. They walk where he walked, and give thanks for his sacrifice.

The Importance of Jerusalem: Judaism

Jerusalem is important to Jews for many <u>religious</u> and <u>historical</u> reasons.

Jerusalem has been part of Jewish History for Centuries

The <u>Tenakh</u>, or Hebrew Bible, mentions <u>Jerusalem</u> several times.

1) 1 Kings chapters 7-8 describes how <u>King Solomon</u> built the Temple and brought <u>together</u> the people of Israel to <u>dedicate</u> it to G-d.

2) <u>Psalm 48</u> tells how G-d chose Jerusalem to be his <u>holy city</u> forever. <u>Psalm 137</u> is a <u>sad</u> song sung by captured Jews to <u>remember</u> Jerusalem.

3) Many of the daily Jewish <u>prayers</u> also talk about Jerusalem. For example, the <u>amidah prayer</u> and prayers used when giving <u>thanks for meals</u>.

> "Great is the Lord, and most worthy of praise, in the city of our God, his holy mountain."
> Psalm 48:1 NIV

Certain places in Jerusalem are particularly Important to Jews

1) The place where the <u>Jewish Temple</u> used to be before it was destroyed by the Romans is now occupied by the <u>Al-Aqsa Mosque</u> (see p.116).

2) However the <u>Western Wall</u> of the Temple is still there. It's a place of pilgrimage and prayer for Jews. Each year large crowds go there on the <u>anniversary</u> of the destruction of the <u>Temple</u>.

3) The <u>Shrine of the Book</u> in Jerusalem contains some of the oldest known Jewish religious writings, called the <u>Dead Sea Scrolls</u>. The scrolls were written over several centuries, starting in about 400 BCE, and were <u>discovered</u> near Jerusalem in the 1940s and 1950s.

4) Many Jews visit the <u>Yad Vashem Holocaust History Museum</u> in Jerusalem in order to remember the <u>six million</u> Jews who were murdered by the Nazis during the <u>Holocaust</u> (see p.106).

The Western Wall is an important prayer site for Jews.

Jerusalem has been a sacred Jewish place for thousands of years

Jewish people consider Jerusalem to be part of the Promised Land, so it will always be important to them. Remember the main areas that pilgrims visit and why they're important.

The Importance of Jerusalem: Islam

Muslims call Jerusalem "Al-Quds", which means "The Sacred Place".

Muhammad Visited Jerusalem in the Night Journey

1) The angel Gabriel was said to have taken Muhammad to Jerusalem and then to Heaven, where he talked to other prophets and saw signs sent by Allah (God).

2) This is called the miracle of Isra (Night Journey) and Mi'raj (rising to Heaven).

3) Because of the Night Journey, Jerusalem is the third holiest place for Muslims after Makkah and Madinah (see p.113).

4) Muslims used to pray in the direction of Jerusalem, but today they pray towards Makkah.

5) Jerusalem also played a part in the lives of the prophets who lived before Muhammad:

> - Abraham's faith was tested by God in Jerusalem — he showed that he was prepared to sacrifice his son.
> - Moses died before he could lead his people to Jerusalem.
> - Jesus died in Jerusalem (see p.117).

Muslims don't believe that Jesus was the son of God, but they do believe he was one of the prophets.

The site of the Al-Aqsa Mosque is Special to Muslims

1) The Qur'an calls the place in Jerusalem where Muhammad was taken during the Night Journey "the Farthest Mosque". Most Muslims believe this to be where the Al-Aqsa Mosque now stands.

2) Most Muslims believe the exact place from where Muhammad was taken to Heaven is the "Rock". This is found in the beautiful gold-domed building — the Dome of the Rock — near the Al-Aqsa Mosque.

3) Many Jews and Muslims also believe this sacred rock is where the prophet Abraham was ready to sacrifice his son Ishmael when God asked him to.

The Dome of the Rock is situated near the Al-Aqsa Mosque.

Jerusalem is the third holiest place to Muslims

Muhammad's Night Journey to Jerusalem makes Jerusalem a special place to Muslims. If you can remember the different places that are linked to his visit, then you can't go too far wrong.

Conflicts in Jerusalem

Jerusalem is sacred to different <u>religions</u> — this has resulted in many <u>conflicts</u> over the years.

Jews, *Muslims* and *Christians* have all wanted to *Rule Jerusalem*

1) Many <u>Jews</u> were <u>driven out</u> of Israel by the Romans around 66 CE (see p.115), but they still believed that Israel was the land God had <u>promised</u> to them.

2) Later, Israel came under <u>Muslim</u> rule and became known as <u>Palestine</u>. The <u>Arabs</u> living in Palestine were just as sure that it was their country as the <u>Jews</u> were.

3) <u>Christian Crusaders</u> also made several attempts to rule Jerusalem — one resulted in the Al-Aqsa Mosque <u>temporarily</u> being made into a <u>church</u> and a palace (see p.116).

The Palestinian-Israeli *Conflict* *is* *Ongoing*

In modern times there has been conflict between <u>Palestinian Arabs</u> (mostly <u>Muslims</u>, but some <u>Christians</u> too) and <u>Israeli Jews</u>:

- **1897** — Many Jews wanted to return to <u>Palestine</u> to form their <u>own nation</u>, rather than live as a persecuted minority. The <u>Palestinians</u> already living in Palestine <u>did not like this idea</u>.

- **1939-45** — <u>World War Two</u>. The <u>Holocaust</u> made the Jews determined to have their own country where they could be <u>safe</u>.

- **1947-48** — There was a <u>war</u> within Palestine after the UN voted to split the nation into <u>separate</u> Arab and Israeli states.

- **1948** — After the <u>war</u>, Jerusalem was <u>divided</u>. <u>Temple Mount</u> (where the Western Wall is situated) was held by <u>Jordan</u> (the Arabs), and Jews were not allowed to <u>pray</u> there.

- **1967** — In the <u>Six-Day War</u>, Israel took over all of Jerusalem. <u>Jews</u> were now able to <u>pray</u> at the Western Wall again.

- Over the following <u>twenty years</u>, there were many bomb <u>attacks</u> against Israel by the <u>Palestine Liberation Organisation</u> (PLO) and other groups, and <u>counterattacks</u> by Israel.

- **1987-1991** — In the <u>First Intifada</u> ('intifada' means 'uprising'), the <u>Palestinians rioted</u> against the Israelis.

- **1991** — A long, complicated <u>peace process</u> began between the <u>PLO</u> and <u>Israel</u>. Eventually the <u>Palestinians</u> got self-government in two areas, the <u>Gaza Strip</u> and the <u>West Bank</u>.

- **2000** — The <u>Second Intifada</u> broke out when the <u>Israeli Prime Minister</u> visited <u>Temple Mount</u> (the Second Intifada ended in 2005). His visit was seen as <u>insulting</u> by Palestinians.

- **2002** — Israel started to build a <u>separation barrier</u> between it and the Palestinian West Bank. Israel claimed it was to keep Palestinian suicide bombers out of Israel.

Palestinians and Israelis both believe that Jerusalem is theirs

Jerusalem's violent history can be a bit tricky to get your head around. So read over this page a couple of times until you understand what happened when, and why it happened.

Peace in Jerusalem

It's not all war — there have been times during the conflict when leaders have agreed to live peacefully.

Egypt and Israel signed a Peace Treaty in 1979

1) The President of Egypt, Anwar Sadat, and the Prime Minister of Israel, Menachem Begin, took part in peace negotiations which resulted in them sharing the Nobel Peace Prize in 1978.

2) They signed a peace treaty between Egypt and Israel in 1979.

3) This agreement made Egypt the first Arab state to officially recognise Israel as a nation.

4) However, not everybody was happy with this agreement. Anwar Sadat's involvement in the Egypt-Israeli peace treaty was one of the factors that led to his assassination by Egyptian extremists.

The PLO and Israel signed a Peace Agreement in 1993

1) The Palestinian leader, Yasser Arafat, led the Palestine Liberation Organisation (PLO), which fought against Israel for many years. In 1993, Arafat and the PLO decided to no longer use violence and accepted Israel's right to exist.

2) Israel's Prime Minister, Yitzhak Rabin, signed a peace agreement with Arafat in 1993, which led to them both being awarded the Nobel Peace Prize in 1994.

3) This was particularly important because the agreement was between two leaders who had previously been at war.

4) Yitzhak Rabin was assassinated in 1995, however, by an Israeli extremist who was angry that Rabin had signed a peace agreement with the Palestinians.

Peace agreements have been signed over the years

Sadly, none of the treaties have led to complete peace in Israel. It's also worth noting that some leaders who have tried to make peace with the opposition have been assassinated by extremists.

Peace in Jerusalem

Many organisations are involved in trying to keep the peace in Jerusalem and surrounding areas.

Religious Organisations *try to help out*

1) Islamic Relief supplies emergency help, education, food and health services to people of all religions and does some of its work in Israel/Palestine.

2) Christian Aid has been helping people in Israel since the 1950s. They work with both Palestinian and Israeli human rights organisations, and try to give everyone access to important resources and services, regardless of their religion.

> Both of these organisations can be controversial. For example, in June 2014 it was reported that the Israeli government believes Islamic Relief has ties with Hamas (a Palestinian group) and has banned it from Israel. However, Islamic Relief said it has no ties with Hamas.

Many other **Volunteer Organisations** *try to encourage* **Peace**

Volunteer organisations and non-governmental organisations are working towards peace:

The Open House project

The Open House project is a peace education centre set up in the town of Ramla (Israel) in 1991. It runs workshops that allow young Arabs and Jews to talk and listen to each other.

Amnesty International

This international organisation works for human rights and the release of political prisoners worldwide. It has campaigned against human rights violations by both sides in Israel and the Palestinian Occupied Territories for many years.

The Parents Circle Families Forum (PCFF)

The PCFF is a group of families, both Palestinian and Israeli, who have had family members killed in the conflict. It promotes peace and reconciliation between the two sides rather than seeking revenge.

There are lots of organisations that promote peace

Well, that was a slightly more positive page. Try to remember who the different organisations are and what they're doing to try to make peace in Jerusalem and the surrounding areas.

Questions

You probably know all about Jerusalem, as well as a few other holy places, by now. Give these questions a go to see which bits you've understood and which bits you should read over again.

Warm-up Questions

1) Name a pilgrimage site for Christians.
2) Why is Makkah important to Muslims?
3) Why do Hindu pilgrims visit the river Ganges?
4) Briefly explain why Jerusalem is important to   a) Christians b) Jews c) Muslims
5) Explain how one person or organisation has worked to promote peace in Jerusalem.

Practice Questions

These questions will give you the chance to show what you've learnt.

1) Copy out the grid below, putting each of the holy places in the correct column.

Christianity	Judaism	Islam	Hinduism	Sikhism	Buddhism

Golden Temple   **River Ganges**   **Sarnath**   **Santiago de Compostela**
Makkah   **Lumbini**   **Western Wall**
Canterbury   **Masada**   **Dome of the Rock**

2) Copy out and complete this passage, adding the correct words from the list below:

gurdwaras   worship   Amritsar   Hinduism

pilgrimages   Sikhism   God   gurus

When he founded _____ , Guru Nanak rejected any aspects of

_____ that he considered to be meaningless, so Sikhs don't generally place

much value in _____ . However, they do visit special _____ or

places that are linked to any of the _____ .

The Golden Temple, situated in the holy Sikh city of _____ , is one of the most

important places for Sikhs to visit. It is where the original Guru Granth Sahib is kept

during the day, so many Sikhs go there to _____ and feel close to

_____ .

3) Name three groups that have ruled over Jerusalem over the years.

Section Eight — Summary Questions

The questions on this page cover the main points from the whole of Section 8. See how many of them you can answer (without peeking). If there are any you're not sure about, have another read of the section, and try again. Then I reckon you'll be due a well-earned rest.

1) What is Yad Vashem? (Judaism)

2) What is the significance of the Hajj to Muslims?

3) What is the significance of the town of Ayodhya to Hindus?

4) Explain why Sikhs are less likely to go on a pilgrimage than members of other religions.

5) Name two places that are considered holy by Sikhs.

6) Name two places that are considered holy by Buddhists.

7) Give two reasons why King David is important to Jews.

8) Why did the Roman authorities order the crucifixion of Jesus?

9) Explain why many Christian holy places are located in Jerusalem.

10) Explain why Christians might visit the Church of the Holy Sepulchre.

11) What is the significance of the Via Dolorosa for Christians?

12) Give two reasons why Jerusalem is holy to Jews.

13) Explain the importance of the Western Wall to Jews.

14) Explain how the story of Muhammad's Night Journey inspired a pilgrimage.

15) What is the importance of the Dome of the Rock to Muslims?

16) Do you think that Jerusalem should still be considered holy after all of the violence that has happened there over the years? Give reasons for your answer.

17) Do you think certain places can be particularly holy? Give reasons for your point of view.

18) Do you think pilgrimages are important for religious believers to demonstrate their commitment to their god? Why? / Why not?

19) Explain how Anwar Sadat and Menachem Begin contributed towards peace in Jerusalem.

20) How did Yasser Arafat and Yitzhak Rabin contribute towards peace in Jerusalem?

21) Describe the work of a volunteer organisation working for peace in Israel.

The Birth of Jesus

Christians believe that Jesus is God's son, so he is a pretty important guy.

Jesus was Born in a Stable

1) Christians believe that Jesus is the Son of God, who lived on Earth around 2000 years ago. The story of his birth was written in the gospels of Matthew and Luke. This story is known as the nativity.

2) Jesus's mother, the Virgin Mary, was visited by the angel Gabriel, who told her that she would give birth to the Son of God. This worried her because she was not yet married to Joseph, but she trusted God's decision.

3) When Mary was heavily pregnant, she travelled with Joseph from Nazareth to Bethlehem to register for a census.

4) There were no free rooms available in Bethlehem, so Mary and Joseph had to stay in a stable. This was where Jesus was born — they laid him in a manger (an animal's feeding trough) to sleep.

5) That night, an angel appeared to a group of shepherds in a field near to Bethlehem. The angel told them that a saviour had been born and they could find him sleeping in a manger. The shepherds hurried to worship the baby Jesus.

6) Then some wise men saw a bright star in the sky which symbolised the birth of a new king. They followed the star, which led them to Jesus, and they gave him gifts of gold, frankincense (a type of incense) and myrrh (a perfume).

Jesus's birth was Predicted

1) There are many prophecies (predictions) in the Old Testament of the Bible which refer to the birth of a Messiah (a saviour). The descriptions of Jesus's birth in the gospels fulfil these prophecies.

> Jews don't believe that Jesus was the Messiah.

2) One prediction was that "The virgin will conceive and give birth to a son" (Isaiah 7:14 NIV) — according to Matthew's account of Jesus's birth, this came true.

3) There are also Old Testament passages which are interpreted in the New Testament as prophesying the life, crucifixion and resurrection of a Messiah.

4) Christians believe that Jesus was the Messiah — a saviour who lived on Earth so that he could die to gain forgiveness for the sins of all of humankind. He rescued humankind by his death so that all those who have faith in him could go to Heaven.

5) Jesus becoming a human form of God himself (or a human version of 'the Word' of God) is known as the Incarnation.

> "The Word became flesh and made his dwelling among us." John 1:14 NIV

Christians believe that Jesus was the Messiah who rescued mankind

There are lots of prophecies about a Messiah in the Old Testament, so they knew he'd be coming one day. But don't forget that Jews don't see him as the Messiah though.

The Significance of Christmas

Christmas is celebrated in many different countries. The original reason for the celebration was to remember the birth of Jesus, but people celebrate it for various reasons today.

Christmas is a Celebration of Jesus's Birth

1) Most Christians celebrate Christmas — it marks the birth of Jesus, who they believe was the incarnation of God (see p.125). The exact date of his birth is unknown, but it's usually celebrated on December 25th.

2) Christians believe Jesus was the Messiah, so his birth is considered a special event that deserves celebration. They believe that he had the power to save the whole human population, even those who weren't born yet.

3) Christmas is important because it's a time when Christians remember Jesus's birth, and give thanks to God for sending him to save them.

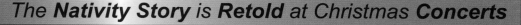

The Nativity Story is Retold at Christmas Concerts

1) Today, children often retell the story of Jesus's birth (the nativity story) in a Christmas concert. This reminds Christians why they're celebrating Christmas.

2) A nativity scene is often set up to decorate churches and homes. This includes the manger full of straw where Jesus slept.

3) There are also special Christmas church services which include carol singing (singing Christmas songs). Some Christians go to Midnight Mass on Christmas Eve to mark the start of Christmas Day.

4) Christmas is often celebrated with a big family meal and an exchange of presents. Giving and receiving presents reminds Christians that Jesus was a gift to them from God. It also reminds them of the presents that the Wise Men brought Jesus in Bethlehem.

5) Some Christians also mark Advent — the period leading up to Christmas. It begins four Sundays before 25th December and is a period of waiting and preparation for the main celebration.

Christmas is a celebration of the birth of Jesus Christ

Christmas is an important celebration for Christians. More and more emphasis is being placed on giving gifts, but Christians try to remember that Jesus himself is the most important gift.

Love and Christianity

Love is central to the Christian faith.

God showed his Love by Sending Jesus

1) Christians believe that God expressed his love for them by sending his son — Jesus.

2) Christianity believes that Jesus was crucified on our behalf to save us from our sins.

3) Christians think that if they repent their sins (are sorry, seek forgiveness and try hard not to repeat them) they will be forgiven. This will lead to their salvation, and they will be given eternal life.

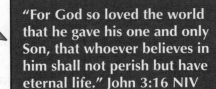

"For God so loved the world that he gave his one and only Son, that whoever believes in him shall not perish but have eternal life." John 3:16 NIV

Jesus taught not just to Respect — but to Love

1) Jews who didn't believe that Jesus was the Messiah often accused him of breaking religious laws. For example, he healed people on the Sabbath when Jews were not supposed to do any work.

2) Jesus thought the 'spirit' of the law, however, was more important than following it exactly as it was written. He believed that if you were a good person, you would do good things.

3) He taught that motivation was even more important than actions — being angry with someone could be nearly just as bad as killing them (Matthew 5:21-22).

4) Jesus taught his followers to love — not only their friends and neighbours, but their enemies as well.

Love is a Key Concept in Christianity

1) Christians try to love and care for others in an unconditional and selfless way — this is called agape.

2) Many Christians believe that because Jesus suffered for them, they have a duty to help those who are suffering.

3) In Matthew 25:31-46, Jesus explains that salvation will come to those who show love by helping people in need.

Love and Christianity

Christians believe that love is <u>all-important</u>, and they express this in a number of different ways.

Monks and *Nuns* express their *Love* of *God*...

Monks and nuns express their <u>love of God</u> by <u>dedicating</u> their lives to God and often live together in religious communities. There are <u>two</u> main types of religious community:

Contemplative orders

- Monks and nuns in <u>contemplative orders</u> aim to <u>remove themselves</u> from the world and dedicate their lives to God.
- They spend a lot of time praying, but the rest of their time is usually spent <u>studying scripture</u> or <u>working</u>.

Apostolic orders

Members of <u>apostolic orders</u> also dedicate time to prayer and study, but they also do charity work '<u>in the world</u>'. Examples include the <u>Sisters of Mercy</u>, who are involved in teaching and caring for the sick.

...and *Other People*

1) Those in <u>apostolic orders</u> go out into the community to try to <u>help</u> people and to advance the community's <u>faith</u>. For example, the Roman Catholic Society of Jesus (<u>Jesuits</u>) are famous for their work in <u>education</u>.
2) <u>Mother Teresa</u> was a Roman Catholic nun who founded the <u>Missionaries of Charity</u> in Calcutta, India. The nuns of her order now work to <u>relieve</u> the suffering of the poor all over the world.
3) Members of contemplative orders <u>pray</u> for others and offer <u>spiritual guidance</u> to visitors.

Love of *God* and *Others* is also seen in *Local Churches*

1) Most local churches try to take an <u>active role</u> in the community.
2) One of a church's main functions is to help its congregation <u>express</u> its <u>love of God</u>. This is done by holding regular <u>religious</u> services for people in the local area (parishioners).
3) Some local churches demonstrate their love for others by getting involved in campaigns about <u>social issues</u>, e.g. by raising money to help the <u>poor</u> and <u>underprivileged</u>, or encouraging people to buy <u>fairly traded</u> products.
4) Many churches have <u>youth groups</u> and <u>Sunday Schools</u> to encourage young people to get involved with the Church and its activities.

Christian communities express their love of God and others

Churches get involved in all sorts of activities: church choirs, coffee mornings, Bible study groups, fund-raising... often to express their love of God and of other people.

Jesus and Forgiveness

For Christians, Jesus is the best example to follow in order to know how to treat other people.

Jesus believed in Forgiveness

1) Forgiveness is difficult, and it is often considered to be wrong. But there are many instances in the New Testament where Jesus said it is essential:

- When Peter asked Jesus how many times he should forgive someone who sins against him, Jesus said "not seven times, but seventy-seven times" (Matthew 18:22 NIV).
- In his famous Sermon on the Mount, Jesus taught about forgiveness, tolerance and not retaliating. He said that "If anyone slaps you on the right cheek, turn to them the other cheek also." (Matthew 5:39 NIV)
- John's gospel tells the story of when Jesus met a woman who was about to be stoned to death for adultery. Jesus shocked the Jewish officials by telling them, "Let any one of you who is without sin be the first to throw a stone at her." (John 8:7 NIV)

2) Jesus's attitude towards forgiveness was considered radical by many at the time, but Christians today attempt to follow his example.

Jesus challenged Zacchaeus — a Corrupt Tax Collector

1) Luke chapter 19 describes the story of when Jesus met Zacchaeus — an important tax official.
2) Tax collectors were unpopular figures and were famous for cheating people out of money.
3) Jesus was in the town of Jericho and crowds had gathered to see him. Zacchaeus was a short man, so he had climbed a tree to try to get a good view of Jesus.
4) Jesus shocked the crowd by calling Zacchaeus down from the tree and telling him that he was going to eat at Zacchaeus's house.
5) The crowd was angry because they felt that Jesus shouldn't be mixing with people like Zacchaeus. But after spending time with Jesus, Zacchaeus apologised for his behaviour and promised to repay everyone he had cheated.

> "Here and now I give half of my possessions to the poor, and if I have cheated anybody out of anything, I will pay back four times the amount."
> Luke 19:8 NIV

6) The story shows that everyone should be forgiven if they change their ways — even the most hated outcasts from society.

Jesus challenged people to forgive rather than seek revenge

Jesus taught his followers lots about treating people fairly and trying to forgive them rather than seeking revenge. These principles are still held strongly by Christians today.

St Paul

St Paul wrote roughly <u>half</u> of the books in the <u>New Testament</u>, but he <u>wasn't always</u> a <u>Christian</u>...

St Paul was originally a Roman Jew

1) St Paul was born as <u>Saul</u>, a <u>Roman Jew</u> who was famous for <u>persecuting Christians</u>.

2) Whilst on his way to <u>Damascus</u> in Syria to <u>arrest</u> more <u>Christians</u>, <u>Jesus</u> appeared to him in a <u>vision</u> and asked Paul <u>why</u> he was <u>persecuting him</u> and his people.

3) Saul changed his name to <u>Paul</u> and became a <u>Christian</u>. He changed his <u>beliefs</u> and <u>lifestyle</u> radically.

4) Paul also <u>travelled</u> to many places, <u>founding</u> churches and <u>telling people about Jesus</u>. During this time, he was <u>shipwrecked</u> and put in <u>prison</u> several times.

5) He became a <u>church leader</u>, writing <u>letters</u> to the <u>churches</u> that he had founded across Europe and Asia to <u>encourage</u> Christians to follow Jesus's teachings. Many of his letters survived and can be found in the <u>New Testament</u>.

Paul taught that Everyone is Equal

1) Paul helped to <u>define</u> what being a <u>Christian</u> was — he was one of the <u>earliest</u> Christian <u>leaders</u> and <u>developed</u> lots of <u>Jesus's teachings</u>.

2) He taught that <u>everyone is equal</u> in God's eyes: "There is neither <u>Jew</u> nor <u>Gentile</u> [non-Jew], neither <u>slave</u> nor <u>free</u>, nor is there <u>male</u> and <u>female</u>, for you are <u>all one</u> in Jesus Christ." (Galatians 3:28 NIV)

3) In his <u>letter</u> to the church in Corinth (an ancient city in Greece), Paul said that <u>wicked</u> people <u>inside</u> the church should be <u>removed</u>, but it was not his business to <u>judge</u> people <u>outside the church</u> — "God will judge those outside." (1 Corinthians 5:13 NIV).

4) Paul, like Jesus, also taught that people <u>shouldn't</u> seek <u>revenge</u> and should instead leave <u>punishment</u> to <u>God</u>.

> "Do not repay anyone evil for evil. [...] Do not take revenge, my dear friends, but leave room for God's wrath"
> Romans 12:17-19 NIV

St Paul picked up where Jesus left off

Paul became a Christian in pretty dramatic circumstances, and it completely transformed his life. His experience meant that he risked his life travelling around to tell people about Jesus.

St Paul

St Paul was inspired by Jesus's teaching on love and forgiveness.

Christian Teaching is based around Love

1) Jesus and St Paul both taught that life should be about more than just obeying rules.
2) They taught that God is love, so people should be like God and put God's love into practice.
3) According to Christians, loving other people, including your enemies, is a good way of making sure that you are acting fairly and encouraging justice:

Jesus

"You have heard that it was said, 'Love your neighbour and hate your enemy.' But I tell you, love your enemies and pray for those who persecute you" (Matthew 5:43-44 NIV)

St Paul

"...you yourselves have been taught by God to love each other. And in fact, you do love all of God's family throughout Macedonia. Yet we urge you, brothers and sisters, to do so more and more" (1 Thessalonians 4:9-10 NIV)

4) Both Jesus and St Paul also said that you should try to show love to people in practical ways:

Jesus

"For I was hungry and you gave me something to eat, I was thirsty and you gave me something to drink, I was a stranger and you invited me in, I needed clothes and you clothed me..." (Matthew 25:35-36 NIV)

St Paul

"Let us not become weary in doing good... Therefore, as we have opportunity, let us do good to all people, especially to those who belong to the family of believers." (Galatians 6:9-10 NIV)

Christians try to Fight Injustice in the Modern World

1) Christians believe that they should try to act justly and show God's love to other people — just as Jesus and St Paul did.
2) This includes being loving and forgiving, and treating all people equally, whatever their race, social class or gender.
3) There are many Christian groups and charities that try to promote justice and fight inequality:

- Christian Aid (see p.104) works to fight the injustice of world poverty, and CAFOD is a specifically Roman Catholic charity that does similar work. Both of these charities help people whatever their religion.

- Christians Against Poverty is a charity that helps people who are poor or in debt to recover financially. They believe that as Christians, they should offer practical help to those in need.

Christians try to put God's love into practice and to fight injustice

Loving all people equally is a pretty key theme in the teaching of both Jesus and St Paul, so it's no surprise that there are lots of Christian organisations and charities that try to do that today.

Christian Leaders, Love and Justice

Lots of Christian leaders have been involved in helping the poor and fighting for justice.

Martin Luther King fought for justice for African Americans

1) For much of the twentieth century, African Americans in the USA were treated unfairly, especially in the south.

2) Black people were segregated (separated) from white people in schools, workplaces, cinemas and on public transport. They were also often stopped from voting.

3) Martin Luther King was a black Christian preacher. In 1955-56, he organised a boycott of the buses in the town of Montgomery, Alabama. That meant that black people stopped using the buses until the bus company let white and black people use the buses equally.

4) King continued to organise many other protests. He asked protesters to be peaceful and non-violent, in line with his Christian beliefs.

5) His work played a big part in persuading America to pass laws which ended segregation.

6) Martin Luther King was assassinated in April 1968.

Mother Teresa helped the Poorest of the Poor in India

1) Mother Teresa was born in 1910 in what is now the Republic of Macedonia.

2) Her birth name was Agnes Gonxha Bojaxhiu, but she took Teresa as her religious name when she became a Roman Catholic nun.

3) She went to India as a missionary and worked as a teacher in Calcutta where there were lots of slums. While there, she felt God was calling her to help the country's poor.

4) Teresa founded an order of nuns called the Missionaries of Charity. They work to help those in need, e.g. those who are desperately sick, or starving people who have no family to help them.

5) Mother Teresa did this work until she died in 1997.

6) She won the Nobel Peace Prize in 1979, and may one day be made a saint by the Catholic Church.

7) The Missionaries of Charity continue to help vulnerable, sick, orphaned and elderly people in over 130 countries around the world.

Martin Luther King and Mother Teresa both fought against injustice

Martin Luther King and Mother Teresa helped disadvantaged people in different ways, but the work they did was inspired by their Christian faith and has left a lasting impression.

Other Religious Leaders and Justice

Leaders from many other religions have worked for justice too.

Mohandas Gandhi was an influential Hindu

1) Mohandas Gandhi was a Hindu who used non-violent protest to help India become independent from Britain.

2) He was born into a Hindu merchant family in 1869 in India and later moved to London to study Law.

> Many people refer to Gandhi as Mahatma Gandhi — 'Mahatma' means 'Great Soul'.

3) Gandhi then lived in South Africa for many years, where he saw how white people were mistreating Indians and black people.

4) When he moved back to India, Gandhi decided to oppose the unpopular British rule and campaign for India to become independent.

5) Hinduism teaches the principle of ahimsa (non-violence), so Gandhi protested against British rule in peaceful ways, such as publicly breaking unjust laws and going to prison.

6) He also worked to end the oppression of women and 'untouchables' (people of low status in Hinduism). He wanted Indians of all religions to live together in peace.

7) India became independent in 1947, but Gandhi was assassinated less than a year later.

The Dalai Lama is an important Tibetan Buddhist Monk

1) The Dalai Lama is an important monk and leader in Tibetan Buddhism.

2) Tibetan Buddhists believe that the very first Dalai Lama could have achieved nirvana (see p.91) but instead chose to be reborn on earth to help humanity. There have been 14 Dalai Lamas — each one is thought to be a reincarnation of the previous one.

3) The present Dalai Lama's name is Tenzin Gyatso. He was born in 1935 to a humble family. When he was two years old, he was proclaimed to be the reincarnation of the previous Dalai Lama.

4) In 1951, the Chinese Communist Party took over Tibet. In 1959, there was a failed uprising. The Dalai Lama went into exile in India, where he still lives now.

5) The Dalai Lama says his guiding principles are compassion, harmony between religions and protecting the Buddhist culture of Tibet. As a Buddhist, he believes in opposing Chinese rule without violence.

Gandhi and the Dalai Lama fought for justice for their people

These are two men whose faith meant that they wanted to fight for justice in non-violent ways. Both figures are respected worldwide, and Martin Luther King listed Gandhi as an inspiration.

Law and Justice

Religious beliefs about justice centre around the idea of <u>responsibility</u> — you must <u>answer</u> for the things you do wrong, and take responsibility for the care of others.

Law and Justice are Essential to most societies

1) Most nations believe that establishing <u>laws</u> is the best way to <u>protect</u> people in society.

2) Without law, there's the risk of <u>chaos</u>. With law, people know what they <u>can</u> and <u>cannot</u> do.

3) In the UK, <u>laws</u> are rules made by Parliament and <u>enforced</u> by the courts and the police.

4) Christianity, Islam and Judaism all teach that <u>God</u> has also created laws for us to follow. Some religious believers think that <u>religious law</u> is more important than the <u>laws of society</u>.

5) Where religious law and state law <u>disagree</u>, some believers think it's better to commit a <u>crime</u> to avoid committing a <u>sin</u> (see below).

6) <u>Justice</u> is the idea of each person getting what they <u>deserve</u>, and maintaining what's <u>right</u>. This means punishing the <u>guilty</u> and protecting the <u>innocent</u>.

Crime or Sin — State law versus Religious law

1) For <u>Christians</u>, there's a difference between a <u>sin</u> and a <u>crime</u>. A sin is when a <u>religious</u> law is broken, i.e. when God's teaching is disobeyed. A crime is when the <u>state</u> law is broken.

2) Christians believe that <u>justice</u> is very important, since we are all <u>equal</u> in the eyes of God. Christians have a <u>duty</u> to look after other people, and to try to <u>guide</u> them to do what's right.

> "Therefore, it is necessary to submit to the authorities, not only because of possible punishment but also because of conscience." **Romans 13:5 NIV**

3) Religious people usually believe they should <u>obey</u> state laws <u>unless</u> that involves <u>breaking</u> an important religious law.

4) But Jesus taught that <u>judgement</u> and <u>punishment</u> belong to God. Passing judgement on others when we are not perfect ourselves is seen as <u>hypocrisy</u>.

> "Do not judge, or you too will be judged. For in the same way you judge others, you will be judged, and with the measure you use, it will be measured to you." **Matthew 7:1-2 NIV**

Law and Justice

Judaism and Islam each have their own sets of <u>religious laws</u> that followers try to live by.

Jewish laws are called Mitzvot

1) Justice is a huge part of Judaism — the Torah is filled with details of <u>laws</u>, <u>rewards</u> and <u>punishments</u>.

2) <u>Judaism</u> teaches that Jews should obey the laws of the land they live in, as well as following the 613 mitzvot (religious laws or commandments) in the Torah.

3) <u>Rabbinical courts</u> (<u>Bet Din</u>) exist in many countries to resolve Jewish disputes. In Israel, a Bet Din has <u>legal</u> powers on matters which are closely linked to Jewish <u>religious life</u>.

> "Appoint judges…and they shall judge the people fairly."
> Deuteronomy 16:18 NIV

Muslims try to follow Sharia

1) <u>Muslims</u> have a clear and detailed religious law (<u>Sharia</u>). It tells Muslims how they should <u>worship</u> and generally live their lives. For example, drinking <u>alcohol</u> is not allowed.

2) <u>Sharia law</u> is often the <u>basis</u> for state law in many Islamic countries. <u>Saudi Arabia</u>, for example, includes a lot of Sharia law in its state law.

3) Muslims believe strongly in <u>justice</u>. The Qur'an teaches that Allah is <u>just</u> and merciful, and that Muslims should treat all people <u>fairly</u> and <u>equally</u>.

4) Muslims consider maintaining justice to be part of their role as '<u>Khalifah</u>'— <u>caretakers</u> of Allah's creation.

> Muslims believe that Allah sees all. He will know if you have committed a sin and you will be made to answer for it on the Day of Judgement. A truly repentant sinner, however, will be forgiven.

Sharia law often forms the basis of state laws in Muslim countries

Religious people try to follow the laws of the land that they live in *and* the laws of their religion. Most of the time these two sets of laws are similar — don't steal, don't hurt others...

Religious Peace Organisations

There are lots of <u>religious organisations</u> that work to help promote world <u>peace</u>.

Pax Christi is a Roman Catholic organisation

1) <u>Pax Christi</u> is an international, non-profit organisation working for <u>human rights</u>, <u>disarmament</u> and <u>peace</u>.

2) They believe <u>violence</u> should be <u>avoided</u>, and work towards creating a world where people can live together in <u>harmony</u>.

3) An important part of their work is <u>reconciliation</u> — encouraging groups of people who are in conflict to <u>mend</u> their <u>relationships</u>.

4) The organisation was originally set up to help <u>resolve conflict</u> between French and German citizens following World War Two, when <u>tensions</u> between the two countries were <u>very high</u>.

The JPF is a Pacifist organisation

1) <u>The Jewish Peace Fellowship</u> (or JPF) is a <u>pacifist</u> organisation — this means that they don't believe in <u>war</u> or <u>violence</u>.

2) It was originally founded to help imprisoned <u>conscientious objectors</u> in World War Two. The organisation believes that <u>military action</u> never solves conflicts, and that <u>active non-violence</u> (e.g. <u>negotiations</u>, promoting <u>social justice</u>) is the only way to settle disputes.

> **A conscientious objector is someone who refuses to fight because it goes against their beliefs.**

The Muslim Peace Fellowship promotes Non-violence

1) The <u>Muslim Peace Fellowship</u> was founded in 1994. It is a group of Muslims who want to promote <u>peace</u> and <u>justice</u>.

2) It is dedicated to making the '<u>beauty of Islam</u>' present in the world.

3) The group promotes <u>peace</u> through Islam, and works to bring about changes that make society <u>fair</u> and <u>compassionate</u> to <u>everyone</u>.

Many religions believe that world peace would be brilliant

These are just three examples of religious organisations that are working towards peace. They all believe that the world would be a better place if there were no wars or conflicts.

The Resurrection

The Bible tells the story of Jesus's crucifixion (when he died on the cross) and resurrection (when he rose from the dead).

Jesus was **Crucified** and **Died** at **Golgotha**

1) Jesus was sentenced to death and led to Golgotha where he was crucified (nailed to a cross to hang until he died).

2) A sign was fixed to Jesus's cross that read "The King of the Jews", to record the charge against him. Passers-by threw insults at Jesus, saying that he could save others, but couldn't save himself.

3) Christians believe that it was by dying on the cross that Jesus saved humankind from their sins. They believe that God had placed all the sins of the world on Jesus while he hung on the cross.

4) In his suffering, Jesus cried out, "My God, my God, why have you forsaken me?" (Mark 15:34 NIV). As he died, the curtain of the Temple tore in two. A Roman soldier said, "Surely this man was the Son of God!" (Mark 15:39 NIV)

5) Jesus's body was taken down from the cross and buried in a tomb cut from the rock, with a stone rolled over the entrance.

Then on the **Third Day** he was **Resurrected**

1) According to Mark, three women, including Mary Magdalene, went to Jesus's tomb to anoint his body.

2) They found the stone had been rolled away from the entrance, and the tomb was empty. A young man dressed in white was there who told them: "He has risen! He is not here. See the place where they laid him. But go, tell his disciples and Peter, 'He is going ahead of you into Galilee...'" (Mark 16:6-7 NIV).

3) The three women fled in terror and didn't say anything to anyone. The oldest copies of Mark end here.

4) Later copies of Mark go on to say that the resurrected Jesus appeared to Mary Magdalene, and then to the eleven remaining apostles. He told them to "preach the gospel to all creation" (Mark 16:15 NIV).

5) Christians believe that Jesus's resurrection was physical, not just spiritual. The risen Jesus wasn't a ghost — he rose again in the flesh, showing God's power over death.

> "He said to them, 'Why are you troubled, and why do doubts rise in your minds? Look at my hands and my feet. It is I myself! Touch me and see; a ghost does not have flesh and bones, as you see I have.'"
> Luke 24:38-39 NIV

Christians believe that Jesus's death saved them

You might have heard parts of this story before, but make sure you read this page properly so you take in as many of the details as possible — it's a really important part of Christianity.

The Importance of the Resurrection

Resurrection means 'coming back to life' or 'rising from the dead'.

Christians believe that **Jesus** was **Resurrected**

1) The Gospels of Matthew, Mark, Luke and John have detailed descriptions of how Jesus met with his followers after he'd risen from the dead.

2) There are stories of Jesus talking to his followers, giving them instructions for the future and eating with them.

3) Christians believe that prophecies in the Old Testament predicted that the resurrection would happen.

4) St Paul said that if the resurrection wasn't true, then Christianity would be pointless.

> **"And if Christ has not been raised, our preaching is useless and so is your faith." 1 Corinthians 15:14 NIV**

Christians believe the **Resurrection** of Jesus **Changed Everything**

1) Christians believe that God raised Jesus back to life, conquering sin and death.

2) The Bible mentions other people who have been raised from the dead, e.g. Lazarus in John, chapter 11. But unlike Jesus, these people all went on to die again in the natural way.

3) Christians believe that Jesus coming back to life after death and then going to Heaven is a promise that anyone can have eternal life in Heaven after death.

> **"Jesus said to her, 'I am the resurrection and the life. The one who believes in me will live, even though they die'." John 11:25 NIV**

4) Jesus's resurrection proved that he had not been defeated by the crucifixion — it showed that he was, in fact, God's son.

The resurrection of Jesus means Christians can go to Heaven

The Bible says that humankind doesn't deserve to go to Heaven because of all the bad things humans do. But Jesus's death and resurrection makes it possible for them to go to Heaven.

The Importance of Easter

Christians celebrate the <u>resurrection</u> of Jesus at <u>Easter</u>.

Easter celebrates Jesus's Rising from the Dead

1) <u>Easter</u> is one of the most important <u>Christian festivals</u>.

2) Christians around the world <u>celebrate</u> Easter in <u>different ways</u>.
   Nearly all of them go to <u>church</u> on <u>Easter morning</u>.

3) The period before Easter is called <u>Lent</u>. During Lent, many Christians <u>fast</u> (<u>eat less</u> than usual and have only <u>simple food</u>). They <u>stop fasting</u> on <u>Easter Sunday</u>. In many countries, such as Ethiopia and Greece, people eat a meal of <u>lamb</u> and <u>bread</u> to celebrate.

4) It's traditional in <u>Russia</u> and other <u>Orthodox Christian countries</u> to <u>greet</u> people on Easter morning by saying "<u>He is risen</u>". People then reply with "<u>Truly, he is risen.</u>"

5) In many places across the world, such as Mexico, Germany and the UK, people put on <u>traditional plays</u> showing Jesus's death and resurrection — these are known as <u>passion plays</u>.

There are lots of Symbols associated with Easter

The symbols associated with <u>Easter</u> are about <u>new life</u> and <u>hope</u>:

Empty cross

An image of the cross <u>without Jesus</u> on it shows that Jesus is <u>no longer dead</u>.

Empty tomb

The <u>tomb</u> is shown to be <u>empty</u> because <u>Jesus</u> has <u>left it</u> and is <u>alive</u>.

Lamb

Jews traditionally <u>sacrificed lambs</u> to God, so lambs symbolise <u>Jesus's sacrifice</u>.
Lambs are also <u>born</u> in <u>spring</u>, often close to Easter, so they symbolise <u>new life</u>.

Eggs

Eggs symbolise <u>new birth</u>, and a <u>chick</u> breaking out of its <u>egg</u> reminds some people of <u>Jesus</u> breaking out of his <u>tomb</u>. In some countries, they <u>paint</u> Easter eggs <u>red</u> to symbolise the <u>blood</u> Jesus shed when he <u>died</u> on the <u>cross</u>.

Sunrise

A sunrise brings <u>light</u> after <u>darkness</u>, so it's a symbol of <u>hope</u>.

Easter celebrates the hope that Jesus's resurrection brings

For Christians, the resurrection of Jesus is one of the most important events in the Bible, and that's why it's celebrated at Easter. Try to remember some of the Easter symbols.

Questions

It's the end of Section 9, and you've made it to the end of the book — congratulations.
But just before you run off to celebrate, there are some lovely questions to get stuck into.

Warm-up Questions

1) Describe one thing that a Christian might do to celebrate Christmas.
2) What is agape?
3) Name one thing that people living in contemplative orders do.
4) Which denomination of Christianity is Pax Christi connected with?
5) Who said that if Jesus's resurrection didn't happen then Christianity is pointless?

Practice Questions

These practice questions are a great way to practise what you've learnt — the clue's in the name.

1) Copy out and complete this passage, adding the correct words from the list below:

   nativity   humankind   prophecies   incarnation   virgin   saviour

   a) Christians believe that Jesus is their _____, a Messiah sent from God so that
   the sins of _____ can be forgiven.

   b) The story of Jesus's birth fulfils _____ which were made in the Old Testament.
   These include the fact that Jesus's mother was a _____ when she gave birth.

   c) Christians believe that Jesus was both the Son of God and an _____ of God
   himself. His birth is often called the _____.

2) Are these sentences about religious leaders true or false?
   a) St Paul wrote some of the books in the New Testament.
   b) Martin Luther King believed in protesting peacefully.
   c) Mother Teresa was born in India.
   d) Gandhi was involved in campaigning for Indian independence from Britain.
   e) The Dalai Lama is an important Sikh monk.

3) Copy and complete the passages below using the correct choice of words.
   There are many religious organisations which fight against **(justice / injustice)**. The JPF
   is a **(Jewish / Hindu)** organisation that believes conflicts should be resolved using
   (violent / non-violent) methods. The Muslim Peace Fellowship campaigns for
   peace and tries to change society so that it is **(fair / challenging)** for everyone.

4) Explain why an empty tomb symbolises Easter for Christians.

Section Nine — Summary Questions

Now it's time to really test how much of the information from this section has stuck in your mind. Give these questions a go without flicking back through the pages of the section. If there are some that you just can't manage, have a look at the relevant pages — the answers are all there.

1) How did the Virgin Mary find out that she was going to have a baby?

2) Why was Jesus born in a stable?

3) How did the Wise Men know to go and find the baby Jesus?

4) What do Christians believe will happen if they repent of their sins?

5) Give two reasons why love is an important value to Christians.

6) Give two examples of apostolic orders.

7) What was Jesus's message when he told his followers to "turn to them the other cheek"?

8) Who was Zacchaeus? How did his life change after he met Jesus?

9) What was St Paul originally called? When did he change his name?

10) Give an example of a Christian charity that fights injustice, and explain how it does so.

11) Which group of people did Martin Luther King want justice for?

12) Describe the work of the Missionaries of Charity.

13) How did Mohandas Gandhi's faith influence the way he campaigned?

14) For Christians, what is the difference between a sin and a crime?

15) What is the role of Bet Din in Jewish communities?

16) What is Sharia?

17) Why was the Jewish Peace Fellowship originally founded?

18) What happened to the curtain at the Temple in Jerusalem when Jesus died?

19) According to Mark, who found Jesus's empty tomb on the third day after his death?

20) According to Mark's gospel, what did Jesus tell his apostles to do when he appeared to them after his resurrection?

21) What do Christians believe Jesus's resurrection means for their ability to enter Heaven?

22) Give an example of how a Christian might celebrate the festival of Easter.

23) "Christians shouldn't eat Easter eggs, because eggs have nothing to do with Easter." Explain why a Christian might disagree with this statement.

24) "Christianity is all about loving and worshipping God." Discuss this statement, including different points of view and your own viewpoint.

Section One — Looking for God

Page 10

1) Aesthetic truth — Romeo and Juliet get married.

Historical truth — Elizabeth I was a protestant queen.

Religious truth — God is everywhere.

Moral truth — It's wrong to hurt others.

Scientific truth — Copper conducts electricity.

2) The correct words, in order, are: cosmological, 'First Cause', God, explosion, religious people, the Big Bang

3) E.g. Some religious people believe that God put us on Earth to look after his creation.

4) The words should be in this order: extraordinary, Miracles, scriptures, revelations, proof, healing

Section Two — Key Religious Figures

Page 26

1) **Vyasa** — Hinduism

Muhammad — Islam

Moses — Judaism

Guru Nanak — Sikhism

2) The words should be in this order: Jewish, freedom, Moses, laws, societies

3) Any three of the following: don't harm any living thing; don't take anything you were not given; don't have sex with anyone other than your husband or wife; don't lie or gossip; don't take drugs or drink alcohol.

4) a) false   b) true   c) true   d) false

5) E.g. Vyasa wrote the Mahabharata to make it easy for all Hindus to understand how they should live. I think it is useful to Hindus because it helps them understand how the principles of dharma, karma and moksha fit into their daily lives.

Section Three — Beliefs and Practice

Page 41

1) The words should be in this order: one, creator, omnipotent, omniscient, Trinity, omnipresent

2) a) true   b) false   c) false   d) true

3) It symbolises the three main aspects of Brahman — creator, preserver and destroyer.

4) a) A small comb which symbolises the need to be clean and self-disciplined.

b) A steel bracelet which symbolises strength, honesty and God's eternal nature.

c) Cotton underwear which symbolises the importance of chastity and self-control.

5)

Christianity	Islam	Judaism
ichthus advent candles cross	star and crescent	tallit Torah

Hinduism	Sikhism	Buddhism
Om murti	nishan sahib karah parshad khanda	dharmachakra

Pages 65-66

1)

Christianity	Hinduism	Islam
10 Commandments New Testament gospels	Vedas Bhagavad Gita Ramayana	Hadith surahs Sunnah Sharia law Bismillah

2) a) A collection of Jewish teachings that has been written down over centuries, including the Talmud.

b) The original name of the Sikh Guru Granth Sahib, before it became a guru.

c) The earliest collection of Buddhist writings based on the teachings of the Buddha.

3) The words in order should be: Pillars, muezzin, wudu, Allah, Makkah, Muhammad

4) Prayer is a conversation with God, but meditation involves thinking deeply about God.

5) The correct words, in order, are:

a) Christians, more, death

b) Sikhism, three, Tan, langar

c) Hindus, dharma, ten, niyamas

6) A vocation is a job or role that a Christian believes God has called them to do.

7) The days should be in this order: Shrove Tuesday, Ash Wednesday, Palm Sunday, Maundy Thursday, Good Friday.

8) a) Diwali — Hinduism, Sikhism

b) Hanukkah — Judaism

c) Easter — Christianity

d) Eid ul-Adha — Islam

9) i) d   ii) c   iii) a   iv) b

10) You could have written about Parinirvana Day, Wesak, Magha Puja or others.

E.g. Parinirvana Day marks the death of the Buddha — when he was freed from the cycle of rebirth. It's celebrated by chanting and meditating at the temple.

E.g. Wesak celebrates the Buddha's birthday and his enlightenment. In some forms of Buddhism, it also remembers his death. Buddhists celebrate by decorating their homes and attending the temple.

E.g. Magha Puja is in memory of when 1250 disciples visited the Buddha without being called. It is often celebrated with candlelit processions around the main hall of the temple.

Section Four — Places of Worship

Page 78

1) a) iv   b) v   c) iii   d) ii   e) i

2) a) false   b) false   c) false   d) true

3) The words should be in this order:

    a) gurdwara, langar, statues   b) peaceful, stupa, pagoda

    c) mandir, murti

Section Five — Rites of Passage

Page 92

1) a) Becoming a Bar/Bat Mitzvah is important for a young Jew because it means that he/she is now considered an adult and is responsible for his/her own actions.

    b) An adult baptism welcomes the adult to the Church, whereas a confirmation demonstrates the beliefs of somebody who is already a member. Baptism involves water, whereas confirmation does not.

2) The words should be in this order:

    a) funeral, bereaved, deceased

    b) Christians, resurrected

    c) Prayers, support

3) Muslims believe that when they die, Allah will judge whether they should go to Jannah (Paradise) or Jahannam (Hell). This means that many Muslims try to live obediently so that they please Allah and have their souls sent to Paradise.

4) The correct words, in order, are: Sikhs, reincarnation, life, previous, good, rewarded, reborn

Section Six — Religion and Nature

Page 100

1) The words should be in this order:

    a) animals, humankind, benefit

    b) abused, Noahide, cruelty, Jews

    c) appointed, meat, slaughtered

2) a) Sikhs believe that we are all connected to the environment, so it is in our own best interests to take care of the Earth and all of Waheguru's creation.

    b) Hindus believe in reincarnation, so they think they should respect the Earth so that it's in good condition when they return in a different life.

    c) Buddhists believe in respecting the Earth because they don't think it's fair to cause problems for future generations. They also believe in the unity of nature — humans are a part of nature.

Section Seven — Suffering

Page 111

1) The correct words, in order, are: suffering, test, help, charities

2) a) Christian Aid is a charity which helps people living in poverty, as well as those affected by natural disasters. They set up development projects in developing countries.

    b) JCORE is a Jewish organisation that campaigns for the rights of asylum seekers and immigrants. They offer asylum seekers and immigrants practical help and information.

    c) Islamic Aid is a Muslim organisation which helps people living in poverty. In the UK, the group helps to improve links between Muslims based in the UK and those based elsewhere. They do this to raise awareness of injustice and poverty in developing countries.

3) 1. The truth of **suffering** (dukkha)

    2. The truth of the **cause of suffering** (samudaya)

    3. The truth of **freedom from suffering** (nirodha)

    4. The truth of the **path** to freedom from suffering (magga)

4) Buddhism suggests that there are several different types of suffering, including the natural suffering of illness and getting older; and the disappointment experienced when something doesn't live up to expectations or when something pleasurable ends.

Section Eight — A Holy Place: Jerusalem

Page 123

1)

Christianity	Judaism	Islam
Santiago de Compostela Canterbury	Western Wall Masada	Makkah Dome of the Rock

Hinduism	Sikhism	Buddhism
River Ganges	Golden Temple	Sarnath Lumbini

2) The words should be in this order: Sikhism, Hinduism, pilgrimages, gurdwaras, gurus, Amritsar, worship, God

3) Any three of the following: the Jews, Babylonians, Greeks, Romans, Muslims, Christian Crusaders, Palestinians and Israelis.

Section Nine — More Religious Beliefs

Page 140

1) The words should be in this order:

    a) saviour, humankind   b) prophecies, virgin

    c) incarnation, nativity

2) a) true   b) true   c) false   d) true   e) false

3) The correct words, in order, are: injustice, Jewish, non-violent, fair

4) An empty tomb symbolises Easter because Christians believe Jesus was resurrected from the dead, and left behind an empty tomb three days after his crucifixion.

Glossary

It'd be <u>useful</u> for you to learn these <u>key terms</u> and <u>definitions</u>.

adhan	The Muslim <u>call to prayer</u>, traditionally announced from the top of the <u>minaret</u> by a <u>muezzin</u>.
Adi Granth	The original name for the <u>Guru Granth Sahib</u>, before it was made a <u>guru</u>.
adult baptism	<u>Baptism</u> carried out when the person is <u>old enough</u> to make their <u>own choice</u>.
agnosticism	The belief that there is <u>no way of knowing</u> whether a god (or gods) <u>exists or not</u>.
Al-Aqsa Mosque	A <u>mosque</u> in Jerusalem where Muslims believe <u>Muhammad's journey</u> to <u>Heaven</u> began.
apostolic orders	Groups of <u>monks and nuns</u> who do <u>charity work</u> 'in the world' as well as praying and studying.
aqiqah (or aqeeqah)	A Muslim <u>celebration</u> that takes place <u>seven days</u> after a child is born.
Aron Kodesh	The <u>cupboard</u> in a synagogue which holds the <u>Torah</u>. Also known as the <u>Ark</u>.
asylum seeker	A person who <u>seeks refuge</u> in another country due to <u>fear</u> of racial, religious or political <u>persecution</u>.
atheism	The belief that a god (or gods) <u>doesn't exist</u>.
baptism	The Christian ceremony of <u>entering</u> into the faith which symbolises the <u>washing away of sin</u>.
Bar / Bat Mitzvah	Jewish coming of age ceremonies for <u>boys</u> (Bar Mitzvah) and <u>girls</u> (Bat Mitzvah).
the Big Bang theory	The theory that <u>time and space</u> (and eventually everything else) were <u>created</u> in a <u>huge explosion</u>.
Brahman	The <u>one supreme God</u> in <u>Hinduism</u>. He has three main aspects — <u>Brahma</u>, <u>Vishnu</u> and <u>Shiva</u>.
Brit Milah	A ceremony for <u>Jewish baby boys</u> where they are <u>circumcised</u> to show their <u>bond</u> with <u>G-d</u>.
charismatic worship	<u>Worship</u> involving <u>spiritual experiences</u>, such as 'speaking in tongues'.
confirmation	A ceremony where Christians <u>confirm</u> the <u>vows</u> that were made for them at their <u>infant baptism</u>.
contemplative orders	Groups of <u>monks or nuns</u> who live in <u>isolation</u> and <u>devote</u> themselves to <u>prayer</u>.
cosmological argument	A theory saying there must have been some kind of '<u>First Cause</u>' that <u>created</u> the Universe.
cremation	The <u>burning</u> of <u>dead bodies</u>.
crucifixion	A way of <u>killing</u> someone by fixing their body to a <u>wooden cross</u> and leaving them to die.
dedication	An <u>alternative</u> to infant baptism, so children can <u>choose</u> to be <u>baptised</u> themselves later.
deity	A <u>god</u> or <u>goddess</u>.
denomination	A <u>subgroup</u> of a <u>religion</u> which has <u>some</u> of its own <u>beliefs</u> and <u>practices</u>, e.g. Methodism.
design argument	The theory that <u>someone</u> must have <u>designed</u> the Universe because it is so <u>complex</u>.
dharma	The concept of <u>duty</u> in Hinduism — it is a kind of <u>moral code</u>.
dharmachakra	A <u>symbol</u> used in <u>Buddhism</u> — a <u>wheel</u> with <u>eight spokes</u>, representing the <u>Noble Eightfold Path</u>.
enlightenment	The <u>state</u> of complete <u>understanding</u> that <u>Buddhists</u> aim to achieve, like the Buddha did.
evolution theory	The theory that <u>all life</u> on Earth started from <u>simple cells</u>, and <u>humans</u> developed from <u>apes</u>.
fasting	<u>Giving up food</u> (and sometimes drink) for a period of time, usually to <u>focus</u> on <u>God</u>.
Five Ks	The five <u>physical symbols</u> of faith in <u>Sikhism</u>. They are: <u>kesh</u>, <u>kangha</u>, <u>kara</u>, <u>kachera</u> and <u>kirpan</u>.
Five Pillars of Islam	The five main ways for <u>Muslims to know Allah</u> — <u>shahadah</u>, <u>salah</u>, <u>zakat</u>, <u>sawm</u> and <u>hajj</u>.
five precepts	Five <u>rules</u> that all <u>Buddhists</u> try to follow. There are five <u>additional</u> precepts for <u>monks and nuns</u>.
Five Thieves	The five <u>major weaknesses</u> that humans suffer from, according to <u>Sikhism</u>.
forgiveness	The concept of <u>no longer feeling angry</u> towards a person for their <u>mistake</u> or <u>wrongdoing</u>.
Four Noble Truths	The four truths that summarise the <u>Buddha's teachings</u> about how humans can <u>end suffering</u>.
free will	The <u>ability</u> to <u>choose</u> how you <u>behave</u>. Many religions believe that all humans have this.
Gan Eden	The <u>Jewish</u> term for <u>Heaven</u> or Paradise.

Glossary

Gehinnom	A Jewish version of Purgatory, where souls go to be cleansed before moving to Gan Eden.
general revelation	God showing his existence in a way which is available to all people everywhere.
godparents	Friends or family members chosen by Christians to act as spiritual role models for their child.
Golden Temple	A temple in Amritsar, a Sikh holy city, where the original copy of the Guru Granth Sahib is kept.
the Great Renunciation	The point in the Buddha's life when he gave up all pleasures and wealth in his search for truth.
gurpurbs	Sikh festivals which celebrate important dates in the lives of the Gurus.
Guru Granth Sahib	The most sacred text in Sikhism. Sikhs treat it like a living Guru.
Hadith	A collection of the Prophet Muhammad's sayings and teachings which is read by Muslims.
hajj	The pilgrimage to the Muslim holy city of Makkah which all Muslims should complete once.
hijab	A scarf worn by some Muslim women which covers the head and chest.
immanent	Being present in the world, and taking an active role in human life.
infant baptism	Baptism carried out shortly after birth.
Jannah	The Muslim term for Heaven or Paradise.
justice	The concept of each person getting what they deserve, and maintaining what is right.
karah parshad	A sweet dish made of sugar, butter and flour, which is served to visitors to a Sikh gurdwara.
karma	A Sikh, Buddhist and Hindu idea that states that all good or bad actions have reactions.
khalifah	An Islamic term for 'trustee' which means that humans have been left to care for the Earth by Allah.
kippah	A round skullcap worn by Jewish men to symbolise that G-d's intelligence is greater than theirs.
langar	The kitchen attached to a Sikh gurdwara which offers free, simple meals to all visitors.
Lord's Prayer	A prayer which Jesus taught to his followers that is still commonly used by Christians.
madrasah	A school which meets at a mosque and teaches Muslims about Islamic beliefs and practices.
Mahabharata	An important collection of poetry that shows Hindus how they should live.
Makkah	The birthplace of the Prophet Muhammad. Muslims must visit the city at least once in their lives.
mandir	A Hindu temple.
mantra	Words or short phrases which are repeated over and over by believers from several religions.
meditation	A form of deep thinking, where the believer often tries to focus their mind on God.
melas	Festivals and celebrations that commemorate events from Sikh history.
the Middle Way	The balanced lifestyle followed by the Buddha which allowed him to reach enlightenment.
minaret	The tall tower at a mosque, from which the call to prayer is usually broadcast.
minbar	A raised platform in a mosque, from which the imam (Muslim leader) speaks.
minyan	A group of at least ten adults who must be present for a daily prayer service at a synagogue.
miracle	An extraordinary or unexplainable event, which is often attributed to God.
mitzvot	Jewish laws or commandments given to Moses by G-d.
monotheism	The belief in only one god.
Mool Mantar	A Sikh prayer which lists the important qualities of Waheguru (God).
mourning	A period of deep sadness about someone who has died.
muezzin	The man responsible for calling Muslims to prayer five times a day.
murti	An image or statue of a Hindu deity (god or goddess).
ner tamid	The light in a synagogue which is kept alight at all times.

Glossary

Night Journey	The journey in which Muhammad was taken to Jerusalem and then to Heaven by the angel Gabriel.
nirvana	The state of freedom from the cycle of reincarnation which was achieved by the Buddha.
Nishan Sahib	The Sikh flag, marked with the khanda, which flies over gurdwaras.
Noble Eightfold Path	The way of life taught by the Buddha to help his followers try to achieve enlightenment.
numinous experience	An inspiring experience in which someone feels God's presence.
Om	A sacred symbol and sound in Hinduism. Hindus use the sound to help them focus on Brahman.
omnipotent	Having complete power or authority.
omnipresent	Being everywhere at once.
omniscient	Knowing everything — in the past, present and future.
original sin	The belief that humans do some bad things because of Adam and Eve's sin in the Garden of Eden.
pacifism	The belief that war and violence are wrong under all circumstances.
pilgrimage	A journey to a place of religious significance.
polytheism	The belief in more than one god.
prayer	Communicating with God, using words or in silence.
prophecy	A prediction made by someone who has been given information by God.
Purgatory	A place Roman Catholics believe the soul goes to be punished before it can reach Heaven.
rak'ah	A Muslim unit of prayer, involving a series of ritual movements.
reincarnation	The cycle of birth, death and rebirth which Hindus, Buddhists and Sikhs believe in.
religious artefact	A physical item which holds significance for religious believers, e.g. a sacred text or special food.
religious symbol	Something that reminds religious believers of God or an aspect of their faith.
resurrection	Being brought back to life, in a body, by God.
sabbath	A day of rest (Shabbat in Judaism), reflecting the day that God rested after creating the world.
sewa	The Sikh concept of serving others. There are three different types — tan, man and dhan.
Sharia	An Islamic code of law, based on the Qur'an and the teachings of Muhammad.
Shaytan	A devil (also known as Iblis) who tries to lead Muslims away from Allah.
shruti	Hindu scriptures that are believed to have been revealed to holy men by God.
sin	An act that breaks a religious law or disobeys God's will.
smriti	Hindu scriptures that are based on human memories and traditions.
speaking in tongues	The act of speaking in a different, mysterious 'language' when inspired by the Holy Spirit.
special revelation	God giving a message for humankind to a particular person at a particular time.
stewardship	Taking care of the Earth because it is God's creation and should be preserved.
Sunnah	Muhammad's rituals, habits and recommendations which Muslims try to replicate in their lives.
tallit	A prayer shawl worn by some Jewish adults to remind them of their duty to G-d.
tefillin	Two small boxes containing Jewish scriptures, strapped to the wearer's head and arm during prayer.
theism	The belief that a god (or gods) exists.
tikkun olam	The Jewish belief that they should take care of the Earth, the environment and the poor.
transcendent	Being separate from the world, and not actively involved in human life.
Trinity	The Christian belief that the one God has three persons — the Father, Son and Holy Spirit.
Vedas	Ancient Hindu hymns that were revealed directly by God.
wudu	The ritual washing that Muslims must complete before they pray to Allah.

Index

148

Index

L

langar 22, 58, 74, 75
Last Supper 117
law 14, 15, 29, 42, 45, 55,
        127, 134, 135
lectern 68
Lord's Prayer 13, 50, 51
love 12, 16, 31, 55, 127, 128,
        131

M

Madinah 113, 119
madrasah 73
Mahabharata 24, 25, 49
Makkah 16, 17, 33, 53, 62,
        73, 87, 113, 119
mandirs 77
mantras 76, 77
Martin Luther King 132
mass 60, 68, 126
melas 63
menorah 61, 70
Messiah 31, 89, 125-127
Middle Way 18, 19
Midrash 105
minaret 72
miracles 8, 9, 61, 113, 114, 119
mitzvot 44, 56, 135
moksha 25
monks 18, 20, 49, 55, 99, 128,
        133
monotheism 29
Mool Mantar 34
Moses 9, 14, 15, 33, 44, 61,
        86, 119
mosques 17, 53, 72, 73
Mother Teresa 128, 132
mourning 85-87, 104, 113, 137
muezzin 53, 72
Muhammad 16, 17, 33, 46, 53,
        57, 72, 73, 82, 113, 116,
        119
mukti 91
murtis 40, 77

N

nativity 125, 126
natural selection 5
nave 68
ner tamid 70
Newton, Sir Isaac 3
nirvana 19, 20, 91, 110, 114,
        133
Nishan Sahib 38, 74
Noahide Laws 95
Noble Eightfold Path 19, 38, 59,
        110
numinous experiences 3, 7

O

Om 37
omnipotence 30
omnipresence 28, 30, 35
omniscience 30
original sin 80, 84, 103

P

pagodas 76
Palestine 120, 121
Paul, St 130, 131, 138
Pesach (Passover) 15, 40, 61, 117
pilgrimages 15-17, 33, 62, 113,
        114, 117, 118
polytheism 29
Pope 43, 96, 116
poverty 104, 108, 131
prayer 8, 13, 14, 16, 28, 40,
        50-54, 76, 77, 82, 87,
        102, 103, 105, 107,
        113, 118, 119, 128
precepts 20
Promised Land 14, 115, 116
prophecies 42, 125, 138
prophets 13, 15, 16, 33, 44
puja 25, 77
pulpit 68, 69
purdah 23
Purgatory 88

Q

Qur'an 2, 5, 15-17, 46, 47, 73

R

Ramadan 16, 17, 33, 46, 62
Rehat Maryada 54
reincarnation 35, 91, 98, 133
resurrection 13, 31, 60, 85, 88,
        89, 137-139
revelation 7, 8, 16, 17

S

salat 33, 50, 53
salvation 31, 88, 127
Satan (Shaytan) 33, 103, 107
Sat Nam 34
sawm 33
sewa 58
shahadah 33
Sharia law 47, 95, 135
sheloshim 86
Shema 50, 86
Shrine of the Book 113, 118
shruti 49
Siddur 52
sila 59
sin 88, 134

Singh 23
Sisters of Mercy 128
six realms 91
smriti 49
star and crescent 37
Star of David 36, 70
stewardship 6, 96
St Paul 130, 131, 138
stupas 76
suffering 3, 7, 18, 19, 30, 91,
        94, 102-110, 127, 128,
        137
Sunnah 16
synagogues 36, 40, 44, 45, 52,
        70, 71, 83, 86

T

takhat 75
tallit 40, 71, 83
Talmud 44, 45
tefillin 52, 83
Tenakh 44, 45, 118
Ten Commandments 14, 15, 42,
        56, 70
theism 1
Thumb Theory 3
tikkun olam 97
Torah 2, 14, 30, 42, 44, 45,
        56, 70, 81, 83, 135
transcendent 28, 32, 34
Trimurti 35
Trinity 29-31
truth 1, 7, 22

V

Vedas 24, 49
veganism 94
vegetarianism 20, 74, 94, 98,
        99
Virgin Mary 125
Vishnu 24, 35, 98
Vyasa 24, 25

W

Waheguru 21, 22, 34, 48, 54, 98
Watchmaker Theory 3
wealth 18, 64, 103, 104, 108
West Bank 120
Western Wall 113, 116, 118, 120
World to Come 89

Y

Yad Vashem 113, 118
Yom Kippur 56, 61

Z

zakat 17, 33

Index

RHS31